See IRELAND

Belfast

Galway

Dublin

Cork

by Train

Fergus Mulligan

Appletree Press

Contents

First published and printed by
The Appletree Press Ltd,
7 James Street South,
Belfast BT2 8DL
ISBN 0 86281 169 4
© The Appletree Press Ltd, 1986
All rights reserved

Text: Fergus Mulligan
Photographs: courtesy Bord Failte,
Northern Ireland Tourist Board

9 8 7 6 5 4 3 2 1

Cover: Pontoon and Lough Conn,
Co. Mayo

Introduction

For the visitor who doesn't want to do the driving, train travel is the ideal way of seeing Ireland. Fast, comfortable trains operate from Dublin to all the main towns and cities. With an 8 or 15 day rambler ticket at very attractive prices you can train it to Galway, Killarney, Waterford, Cork, Sligo, Westport, Kilkenny and dozens of other places. You can get on and off when and as often as you like. At a small extra charge provincial buses which reach the tiniest villages from Malin Head to Cahirciveen can be included.

Most trains are air conditioned and you can have a meal, a snack or a drink en route while enjoying the constantly changing scenery from the train window.

The mountains of Kerry, the heather-strewn boglands of central Ireland, the charm of Galway Bay and the peaceful beauty of the Yeats country are all at your fingertips. Trains are a great way to meet the locals, so don't be afraid to ask for help if you're lost. The ticket inspector and station staff will be happy to answer any queries.

THE IRISH RAILWAY SYSTEM

The first railway in Ireland opened in 1834 between Dublin and Dun Laoghaire and was followed by a rapid expansion for nearly 80 years producing a dense network of lines. Private transport has taken its toll of railways since then in Ireland and all over the world. Today Córas Iompair Éireann (CIE) has responsibility for rail and bus services in the Republic. Trains between Dublin and Belfast are run jointly by CIE and Northern Ireland Railways.

Among the recent developments in the rail system is the electrification of the Dublin suburban line, the DART, in 1984. On mainline routes Inter-City trains run at speeds up to 90 mph/144 kph.

Most train lines radiate from Dublin and no journey is longer than 4½ hours. In Dublin there are two mainline stations: Connolly Station (Amiens Street, buses 20, 24, 30) for trains to Sligo, Belfast and Rosslare, and Heuston Station (Kingsbridge, buses 24, 79) for Cork, Killarney, Tralee, Limerick, Galway, Waterford and Westport. A special bus (bus 90) runs between all the Dublin stations, mainline and suburban, at regular intervals.

USING THIS GUIDE

This guide is divided into routes with a commentary on items of interest to be seen on the way. Other places of interest within easy access by bus, bicycle or on foot are also described. Check that the train stops at the station you want and that there is a suitable bus connection for your intended destination.

To make the best use of public transport it is worth acquiring bus and train timetables, available from Tourist Information Offices (TIOs) and railway/bus stations. Connections in the more remote regions may be infrequent so check before setting out. TIOs can provide holiday literature, advice on eating out, arrange booking accommodation and give information on public transport.

TRAIN FACILITIES

Many trains have restaurant cars serving full meals or snack cars for sandwiches, drinks etc. Dining while you travel is a pleasurable experience so make the most of CIE catering. Check that your train has the service you require. First class accommodation is provided on the Dublin-Cork and Dublin-Belfast routes only. You can reserve a seat for a nominal charge at railway stations and most travel agents. Bookings close at 17.00 on the day before you intend to travel.

DISTANCES

Distances are given in the guide in miles and kilometres based on the lineside mileposts which appear every quarter of a mile (400 metres approx.). Most are visible even when the train is travelling fast. Some are quite picturesque such as those on the Sligo line which use different geometric shapes to denote the quarters thus:

OPENING HOURS

Inevitably, opening hours may change from year to year. Before visiting a museum, castle or historic site it is worth phoning in advance or checking at the nearest TIO. Most tourist sites close for lunch between 13.00 and 14.00 and stay open longer in summer than in winter. A list of TIOs is given below.

BICYCLES

Bicycles can be hired in many towns on a daily/weekly basis. Ask at the station or at the TIO. They can be brought on all trains, except the DART, for a small charge. Cycling is an excellent way of seeing items of interest which are not easily accessible by bus.

USEFUL INFORMATION AND
TELEPHONE NUMBERS

Principal Railway Stations and Enquiry Offices
Dublin: for all train and bus enquiries (01) 787777
Heuston Station (01) 771871
Connolly Station (01) 742941

Central Booking Office, 59 Upper O'Connell St
    (01) 746301
CIE, 35 Lower Abbey Street (01) 300777

Tourist Information Offices
Listed below are the telephone numbers and opening
months of main TIOs (opening hours are Mon-Fri, 09.00-
18.00; Sat, 09.00-13.00).

Belfast, 53 Castle Street, Belfast 227888
Cork, Grand Parade, (021) 23251
Derry, Foyle Street, Derry 269501
Dublin, Airport, (01) 376387/8
Dublin, 14 Upper O'Connell Street, (01) 747733
Dun Laoghaire, St Michael's Wharf, (01) 804321/
    807048/806547/805760
Galway Aras Failte, Eyre Square, (091) 63081
Kilkenny, Rose Inn Street, (056) 21755
Killarney, Town Hall, (064) 31633
Limerick, The Granary, Michael Street, (061) 317522
Rosslare Harbour, (053) 33232
Shannon Airport, (061) 61664/61604
Sligo, Temple Street, (071) 61201
Tralee, Godfrey Place, (066) 21288
Waterford, 41 The Quay, (051) 75788
Westport, The Mall, (098) 25711

Dublin

Ireland's largest city and the capital of the Republic lies
on the east coast with air and sea links to Britain, Europe
and the USA. The city has an attractive position bounded
to the north by the Howth peninsula and to the south by
the promontory of Dalkey and Killiney hill.

Dublin is mentioned by the Greek geographer Ptolemy,
who called it *Eblana* in AD 140, while *Baile Atha Cliath*
(the Town of the Hurdle Ford) was first settled by the
Vikings in the 9th century. They made their fortifications
near Wood Quay and retained control until defeated by
King Brian Boru at the Battle of Clontarf in 1014. There
are only a few traces of the Viking town, mainly at the
site of the controversial Dublin Corporation offices on
Wood Quay.

Among the historical attractions of the city are the very
fine Georgian streets and squares. Some have suffered the
ravages of speculators but Merrion Square, Fitzwilliam
Square and parts of St Stephen's Green retain much of
their 250-year-old magnificence.

As a modern capital city Dublin has a wide range of
cultural and sporting activities. It is well supplied with

theatres, cinemas, museums, galleries and shops. There is a growing range of international restaurants as well as many providing traditional fare at every price range: prime steaks, succulent hams, fresh seafood and smoked salmon, game, Irish stew, bacon and cabbage and brown soda bread are available in restaurants and pubs in Dublin and all over the country. Last but not least there are Dublin pubs, famed for conversation and a certain dark stout with a white head on it.

Getting around Dublin

CIE operates city bus and train services including the DART (Dublin Area Rapid Transit). Most buses and trains operate from 07.00-23.30 and a wide range of multi-journey tickets is available from CIE. If you plan to spend more than a couple of days in the city these unlimited travel tickets are well worth while. Taxis can be hired on the street, by phone or from ranks all over the city.

Tourist Information

A list of restaurants, cinemas, theatres and guide to what's on is available from TIOs. Hotel and guest house rooms may be booked at the same office. A useful publication is the fortnightly *In Dublin*, available in all newsagents. This lists every possible event in the Greater Dublin area with addresses, phone numbers and other details.

The principal festivals are the Dublin Grand Opera Society spring season (April), the Royal Dublin Society Spring Show (May), the Dublin Horse Show (August), Dublin International Indoor Showjumping (November) and the Dublin Grand Opera Society winter season (December). Check with the TIO for details.

Cathedrals and Churches

St Patrick's Cathedral, Patrick Street, Dublin 2 (buses: 50, 50A) The national cathedral dates from 1190 and is built near the spot where St Patrick is said to have baptised the first Christians. The drop from street level to the entrance way gives some idea of the cathedral's antiquity. The interior contains monuments to a number of famous Irishmen including Jonathan Swift, the author of *Gulliver's Travels*, who was dean from 1713-45 and is buried here. The choir of St Patrick's has a fine reputation. Open Mon-Fri, 09.00-18.00; Sat, 09.00-16.00; Sun, 10.30-16.30.

Christ Church Cathedral, Lord Edward Street, Dublin 2 (buses: 21A, 50, 50A) Just up the hill, Christ Church was founded in 1038 but greatly altered over the centuries; today the transepts are among the oldest parts. The Norman conqueror Strongbow rebuilt the cathedral in 1172 and is buried here. Inside, Christ Church is a delight and beautifully looked after with lovely brass, woodwork and secluded chapels. Open Mon-Fri, 09.30-17.00; Sat, 09.30-16.00 and Sun.

St Audoen's, High Street, Dublin 8 (buses: 21A, 78, 78A, 78B) Built by the Normans in the 12th century and near to Christ Church, St Audoen's is a charming little church with a lovely font and the attractive Portlester chapel. Just down from the church is a segment of the city walls pierced by St Audoen's arch (1215). Above the gate was the meeting place of many of the Dublin trade guilds. West from the church the area has been landscaped as a park with views over the Liffey as far as Phoenix Park.

St Michan's, Church Street, Dublin 7 (buses: 34, 34A) Stark but attractive interior in this 17th-century church where Handel is said to have practised on the organ. The vaults are famous for the rather gruesome mummy-like corpses on display which have been preserved by the unusually dry atmosphere. Tours Mon-Fri, 10.00-12.45, 14.00-16.45; Sat, 10.00-13.00.

St Mary's, Mary Street, Dublin 1 (buses: all cross city routes) Built in 1627 and lying between Capel Street and O'Connell Street, St Mary's is noted for being the church where Wolfe Tone and the dramatist Sean O'Casey were baptised. Very pleasant unadorned interior where John Wesley preached in 1747. Summer, Mon-Fri, 14.00-17.00.

Public Buildings

Old Parliament House, Bank of Ireland, College Green, Dublin 2 (buses: all cross city routes) Construction of the old Parliament building on an unusual corner site began in 1729 based on a design of Sir Edward Lovat Pearce. The House of Commons and the Lords sat here until the Act of Union abolished Parliament in 1800. Since then the building has been owned by the Bank of Ireland. The House of Lords retains its splendour and contains the Mace from the Commons. Guided tours during banking hours: Mon-Fri, 10.00-12.30, 13.30-15.00; open till 17.00 Thurs.

Trinity College, Dublin 2 (buses: all cross-city routes) Founded in 1591, Trinity has a superb position in the heart of the city. Its parks and quiet squares offer a haven of peace. There are numerous fine buildings in the college, notably the Examination Hall, Chapel, the Provost's House and the Old Library which contains the priceless 8th-century illuminated manuscript, the Book of Kells. Guided tours provided by students in summer. Open Mon-Fri, 10.00-17.00; Sat, 10.00-13.00.

Dublin Castle, Dame Street, Dublin 2 (buses: 50, 50A) Dating from the 13th century and built on the site of an earlier fort, Dublin Castle was once the seat of British government in Ireland. The Heraldic Office is a good spot

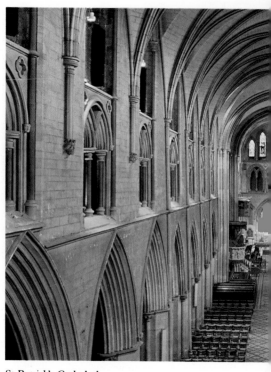

St Patrick's Cathedral

for checking on your pedigree, and the chapel of the Holy Trinity is well worth seeing. Not to be missed are the superb State Apartments used on great social occasions. Guided tours daily. Open Mon-Fri, 08.45-17.00; Sat and Sun, 14.00-17.00.

City Hall, Lord Edward Street, Dublin 2 (buses: 50, 50A, 50C, 56A, 78) Home of Dublin Corporation, City Hall was built 200 years ago as the Royal Exchange. The very imposing entrance hall leads to the chamber containing the city's mace and sword as well as many charters granted to Dublin. Open Mon-Fri, 09.15-16.45.

Leinster House, Kildare Street, Dublin 2 (buses: 7, 7A, 8, 10, 11, 13) The seat of the Irish parliament, Dáil Éireann, was built as the town house of the Duke of Leinster in 1745. Security and other alterations have marred what is a fine building, and the standard of debate is hardly Athenian. Permission to attend from a TD (member of the Dáil), your embassy or by application to the Superintendent's Office. Open when the Dáil is sitting.

General Post Office, O'Connell Street, Dublin 1 (buses:

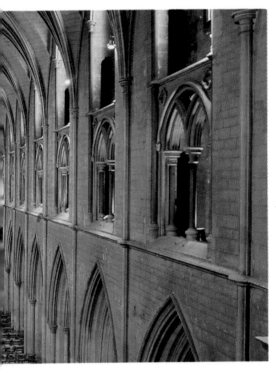

all cross-city routes) First built in 1818 the GPO has a superb façade and was the centre of the 1916 rising. Open daily from early morning to late at night for all postal and telecommunications services.

Four Courts, Inns Quay, Dublin 7 (buses: 24, 51, 79) A very fine example of James Gandon's work, the building dates from 1785 and has an imposing green dome. There is a flurry of legal activity while the courts are sitting and the public are welcome to attend. The first shots in the Civil War of 1922-3 were fired here.

Royal Hospital, Kilmainham, Dublin 8 (buses: 21A, 23, 51, 78, 78A, 79) Recently restored and reopened, this magnificent building dates from 1680 and was a home for old soldiers. It has a delightful courtyard, clocktower and interior surrounded by vast parklands and should not be missed. The corridors have splendid wood panelling and the chapel has some fine plasterwork. The Great Hall is one of Dublin's finest interiors.

Custom House, Custom House Quay, Dublin 1 (buses: all cross-city routes) Many people say this is the most impressive building in Dublin. Built by Gandon in 1791 its pavilions at either end have the arms of Ireland surmounted by a slender dome carrying the figure of Hope. Best seen from across the river, above the railway bridge.

Galleries, Libraries and Museums

National Gallery, Merrion Square, Dublin 2 (buses: 7, 7A, 8) A wide-ranging collection of Irish and European art from all schools. Also has lectures, special exhibitions, library, bookshop and a restaurant. Open daily, 10.00-18.00; Thurs to 21.00; Sun, 14.00-17.00.

National Museum, Kildare Street, Dublin 2 (buses: 7, 7A, 8, 10, 11, 13) Large array of exhibits from the earliest times to recent history including the Ardagh Chalice, Cross of Cong and the Tara Brooch. Open Tues-Sat, 10.00-17.00; Sun, 14.00-17.00.

National Library, Kildare Street, Dublin 2 (buses: 7, 7A, 8, 10, 11, 13) Among the most comprehensive collection of records on every aspect of Irish life including books, periodicals, maps and newspapers. Open Mon-Thurs, 10.00-21.00; Fri, 10.00-17.00; Sat, 10.00-13.00.

Municipal Gallery of Modern Art, Parnell Square, Dublin 1 (buses: 11, 12, 13, 16, 22A) Named after its great benefactor Sir Hugh Lane who died in the *Lusitania*, this gallery has a small but impressive collection of European works of art housed in a delightful Georgian house. Open Tues-Sat, 09.30-18.00; Sun, 11.00-17.00.

Dublin Civic Museum, South William Street, Dublin 2 (buses: 10, 11, 13) Fine collection of items relating to the history of Dublin and environs. Open Tues-Sat, 10.00-18.00; Sun, 11.00-14.00.

Marsh's Library, Patrick's Close, Dublin 8 (buses: 50, 50A, 54, 54A) Founded in 1707 by Archbishop Marsh this is the oldest public library in Ireland and has an excellent collection of old tomes housed in a superb building beside St Patrick's Cathedral. Open Mon, 14.00-16.00; Wed-Fri, 10.30-12.30, 14.00-16.00; Sat, 10.30-12.30.

Natural History Museum, Merrion Square and Merrion Row, Dublin 2 (buses: 6, 6A, 7, 7A, 8) A collection of native birds and other animals from earliest times; frequent exhibitions in the Merrion Row section. Open Tues-Sat, 10.00-17.00; Sun, 14.00-17.00.

Parks and Gardens

Phoenix Park, Dublin 7 (buses: 10, 14, 25, 26) With 1,760 acres this is one of the largest city parks in Europe and has lots of walks, deer and stately mansions. The Zoo is located near the terminus of the 10 bus and has a fine collection of animals from all over the world in near natural surroundings. Open Mon-Sat, 09.30-18.00 summer or sunset in winter; Sun, 12.00-18.00 summer or sunset in winter.

Botanical Gardens, Botanic Road, Glasnevin, Dublin 9

(buses: 13, 19, 34, 34A) Delightful walks among many different types of plants and flowers and trees. Open summer, Mon-Sat, 09.00-18.00; Sun, 11.00-18.00; winter, Mon-Sat, 10.00-16.30; Sun, 11.00-16.30.

St Stephen's Green, Dublin 2 (buses: 10, 11, 13, 14, 15) Haven of peace at the top of Grafton Street with flower beds, lots of wild birds and artificial lakes. Open daylight hours.

Merrion Square, Dublin 2 (buses: 6, 7, 7A, 8) One of the most charming of the inner city parks with a lavish display of colour in summer. Open daylight hours.

Theatres

Abbey and **Peacock**, Lr Abbey Street, Dublin 1, tel. 744505. The National Theatre stages the work of mainly Irish dramatists.

Gaiety Theatre, South King Street, Dublin 2, tel. 771717. The largest theatre in Dublin, with a splendid interior; mixed programmes of drama, musicals, opera and comedies.

Olympia, Dame Street, Dublin 2, tel. 778962. Elaborate 19th-century theatre recently saved from destruction; mixed programme which changes regularly.

Gate Theatre, Parnell Square, Dublin 1, tel. 744045. Puts on the work of Irish and worldwide dramatists.

Project Arts Centre, 39 East Essex Street, Dublin 2, tel. 713327/712321. Avant garde theatre in very informal setting.

In addition to these theatres there are a number of other centres where plays, musicals, etc. are performed. Details of these occasional productions and the numerous cinemas in the city and suburbs can be found in the two evening papers, *Evening Herald* and *Evening Press*, and in *In Dublin* magazine.

Pubs

Much of Dublin's social life centres on pubs which open from late morning to nearly midnight, closing for the famous 'holy hour' between 14.30-15.30. There are over 700 pubs in Dublin; those listed below are only a few of the more noted ones.

Mulligan's, Poolbeg Street, Dublin 2. Famous old pub mentioned by Joyce, with low roofbeams and a good pint; always crowded. **Doheny and Nesbitt's**, Merrion Row, Dublin 2. Frequented by the upwardly mobile or aspirants thereto which is near to **Toner's**, Lr Baggot Street. Lovely old woodwork and mirrors. **O'Donoghue's**, Merrion Row. Noted for traditional music which breaks out spontaneously. **Palace Bar**, Fleet Street, Dublin 2. Once haunted by journalists from the nearby offices, it still has an appealing air. **Neary's**, Chatham Street, Dublin 2. Nice old pub with gas lights, lots of atmosphere and good sandwiches. **Stag's Head**, Dame Court, Dublin 2. Beautiful interior of stained glass and polished wood; serves excellent lunches. **Brazen Head**, Bridge Street, Dublin. Claims to be the oldest pub in Dublin, serving only bottled beer. **Long Hall**, Georges Street, Dublin 2. Fine Victorian pub with glistening bar furniture. **Ryan's**, Parkgate Street, Dublin 8. Near Heuston Station is this delightful pub which is kept in superb order and has escaped vulgar modernisation.

Walks

Dublin is quite a small city and most of the sights mentioned in this section can be reached by a not too strenuous walk from the city centre, taking in the main shopping areas of Grafton Street, O'Connell Street and Henry Street. In addition, Dublin Tourism has devised a series of Tourist Trails around the city which can be covered on your own or with a group. CIE also runs sightseeing trips from Busarus. Details from TIO and CIE.

Darting about Dublin: Howth-Bray

Trains every 5-15 minutes; journey time 1 hour; 23m/ 32km

The DART (Dublin Area Rapid Transit) is the new electric commuter service running around Dublin Bay from Howth on the northside via the city centre to Dun Laoghaire and Bray. Much of the 23-mile route is coastal and gives many different views of the bay. Trains run at 5-minute intervals at peak times and every 15 minutes at other times, from early morning to late at night. The

The Bailey, Howth, Co. Dublin

12

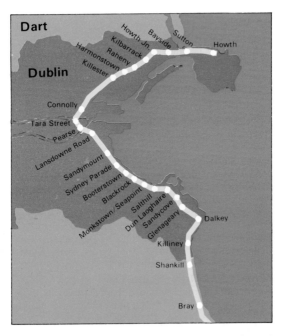

DART is the fastest way of getting around Dublin and the suburbs.

Family tickets for two adults and up to four children are very good value. They can be bought at any rail station. There is also a wide range of weekly, monthly, student and zone tickets covering DART, suburban rail and city bus services. Further information from CIE, 59 Upper O'Connell Street, Dublin 1, tel. 746301

HOWTH
Pretty fishing village recently developed with a yachting marina; a great place to buy fish. Visit the Abbey Tavern for ballads, Guinness and open fires. **Howth Castle** gardens are famous for their luxuriant rhododendrons (May/June) and Ireland's oldest tree planted in 1585 (open all year, 08.00 to sunset). Spectacular walk around Hill of Howth from harbour (signposted) to Sutton station with uninterrupted view of Dublin Bay.

SUTTON

BAYSIDE

HOWTH JUNCTION
The railway line from Belfast and Dundalk joins on the right.

KILBARRACK

RAHENY

HARMONSTOWN

St Anne's Park nearby with superb rose gardens runs down to the sea-front at Dollymount Strand, where a wooden causeway leads to the long arm of the Bull Island, a bird sanctuary with miles of golden sand.

KILLESTER

CONNOLLY STATION (Amiens Street)

Alight for city centre, north side. *See also Dublin-Rosslare chapter.*

TARA STREET

Nearest station for city centre, with O'Connell Bridge two minutes away; alight for O'Connell Street, Grafton Street, Abbey Theatre, cinemas, etc.

Facing the entrance is Gandon's 1591 **Custom House** across the river, now government offices. This is one of Dublin's finest Georgian buildings and worth inspection. It houses many of the records of births, marriages and deaths; useful for ancestor hunters.

PEARSE STATION (Westland Row)

Just before entering the station the line passes above the campus and playing fields of Trinity College, founded in 1591 *(see Dublin chapter).* Pearse Station saw the departure of Ireland's first train on 17 December 1834 for Dun Laoghaire.

LANSDOWNE ROAD

Approaching the station the train passes under the stands of the Irish Rugby Football Union headquarters, venue for regular international matches.

SANDYMOUNT

On Merrion Road are the premises of the **Royal Dublin Society (RDS)** founded in 1731, which hosts the Spring Show (May) and the prestigious Dublin Horse Show (Aug) plus regular concerts, exhibitions and lectures. For information, tel. 680645.

SYDNEY PARADE

The setting for James Joyce's short story *A Painful Case* and the station for the vast expanse of Sandymount Strand. Though covered at high tide, when the tide is out the sand seems to continue over the horizon.

Chester Beatty Library and Gallery of Oriental Art, 20 Shrewsbury Road: one of the finest collections of eastern art, books, manuscripts, paintings, costumes and artefacts in the world. They are the gift of Chester Beatty, the American millionaire. Tues-Fri, 10.00-17.30 excl. lunch and Sat, 14.30-17.30; conducted tours, tel. 692386.

BOOTERSTOWN
Views of Dublin Bay on left from here to Dun Laoghaire.

BLACKROCK
Open air swimming pool (seawater, summer only) and seaside park beside the station.

MONKSTOWN/SEAPOINT
For traditional Irish music in an old style flagged kitchen visit **Comhaltas Ceoltoiri Eireann**, 32 Belgrave Square, tel. 800295

SALTHILL

DUN LAOGHAIRE
Busy suburb and harbour for Holyhead car ferry. Pier walks are nearly a mile (east pier is best) with views of the coast line and Howth from the end. This is also the country's chief yachting centre with spectacular races out in the bay during spring and summer. The **National Maritime Museum** in the old Mariner's Church contains items relating to Ireland's nautical past; Haigh Terrace, summer, Tues-Sun, 14.30-17.30; rest of year, Sun afternoon only.

SANDYCOVE
The **Joyce Museum** in a Martello tower on the sea-front was once the author's home and is the location of the opening scene of *Ulysses*. May-Sept, Mon-Sat, 10.00-17.15; Sun, 14.30-18.00. Other times by arr., tel. 808571. Nearby Forty Foot, a male-only bathing spot much contested by feminists.

GLENAGEARY

DALKEY
The very pleasant town has two medieval castles, Archbold's Castle, 16th-century (key from 59 Castle Street) and Bullock Castle (tel. 886993).
Dalkey Island (boat from Coliemore Harbour, signposted) is tiny and has church ruins, a Martello tower and goats. Superb coastal walks from Coliemore up Vico Road to Killiney.

KILLINEY
Most attractive bay sometimes compared to Naples with hilltop park and wooded walks. Long pebble-strewn beach is ideal for bathing and runs as far as Bray; lovely views from coast road.

SHANKILL

BRAY
Terminus of the DART service but the railway continues to Wexford and Rosslare.

See also Dublin-Rosslare chapter.

Dublin-Rosslare

3 trains per day; fastest journey 2 hours 50 minutes; 104m/166km

The railway line to Rosslare is among the most scenic in the country. Soon after leaving Dublin the train runs along the coast, giving splendid views of the Irish Sea as far as Wicklow town. Then, turning inland, it runs from the idyllic Vale of Avoca to Arklow before reaching the banks of the Slaney and the approach to Wexford to terminate at the international ferryport of Rosslare.

CONNOLLY STATION (Amiens Street)
Former headquarters of the Great Northern Railway (Ire-

Powerscourt House, Co. Wicklow

land) this is a fine Italianate building dating from the 1840s with a graceful façade on to Talbot Street. Alight here for Busarus (country bus station) and north city centre.

From here the line runs above the city to cross the River Liffey giving excellent views to right and left. The train runs non-stop between Connolly and Bray. *For intermediate stations see Darting about Dublin.*

BRAY (14m/22km)

The seaside resort of Bray is a favourite day trippers' destination with its long promenade, fun fair, sea bathing and the atmosphere of a quaint Victorian watering hole. There is safe bathing from the esplanade or from Naylor's Cove beneath Bray Head, the mountain which dominates the south end of the town and from which there are splendid views right across Dublin Bay.

Glen of the Dargle *2.5m/4km.* This is a pretty country

walk beside the River Dargle which runs past Lover's Leap, a prominent rock outcrop overhanging the valley (signposted off the Main Street).

Enniskerry *3m/5km W; bus from Bray*. A delightful village set on a wooded hill beneath the Sugarloaf mountain. Up the hill from the main square is the entrance to the 14,000 acre **Powerscourt Estate**. The 18th-century mansion was gutted in a recent fire but the magnificent terraced gardens are carefully laid out with statues, hedges, miniature lakes, inlaid pavements and unusual trees and shrubs. A curiosity is a graveyard for the numerous family pets. The Powerscourt Waterfall (4m/6.5km from Enniskerry) is over 400 ft/120 m high, making it the highest in the British Isles. The waterfall is open all year; Powerscourt Estate: Easter-Oct, 10.00-17.30.

From Bray-Greystones the railway clings to the cliffside through short tunnels with dramatic sea views to the left. There is also a signposted clifftop walk to Greystones which is well worth taking (5m/8km; start at foot of Bray Head).

Glendalough *St Kevin's bus from Bray, 18m/29km or Stephen's Green, Dublin, 32m/51km; nearest station Rathdrum, 9m/14.5km, but no bus*. Founded in the 6th century by St Kevin, this is a spectacular monastic site in a deep valley. The monastic city and school attracted scholars from all over Europe. Enter by the ancient gateway and follow the path to the round tower, 103 ft/31 m high, still intact with its elevated doorway and conical cap. To the west is St Mary's church with a massive portal and nearby the Priest's House, a 12th-century structure. The high cross is called St Kevin's Cross and dates from the 7th century, while the largest building is the Cathedral. Down near the river is the very attractive church of St Kevin with a miniature round tower/belfry. Further up the valley there are delightful river walks, nature trails and picnic facilities. Glendalough should not be missed.

GREYSTONES (19m/30km)

KILCOOLE (21m/34km)

WICKLOW (30m/48km)

Mount Usher Gardens, Ashford *4m/6.5km NW; bus from Wicklow*. Carefully laid out with riverside walks along the Vartry river and containing many rare and unusual plants and shrubs. Gardens, antique shop and café are open Mar-Sept, Mon-Sat, 10.00-17.30; Sun, 14.00-17.30; tel. (0404) 4116. **Devil's Glen,** *1m/1.5km N of Ashford*. This is an unusual rock formation with a steep 100 ft/30 m fall into the Devil's Punchbowl and walks high up on the cliffside.

RATHDRUM (39m/62km)

A little town nestling prettily high on the Avonmore Valley.

Avondale *1m/1.5km; bus.* The former home of Charles Stewart Parnell, patriot, is now a state park (open all year) with walks, nature trails and picnic spots. Avondale House (1779), now a forestry school, is open May-Sept, 14.00-18.00; tel. (0404) 6111.

Avoca *6m/9.5km S; bus from Rathdrum.* A delightful village famous for the composer Tom Moore's tree at the Meeting of the Waters where the Rivers Avonmore and Avonbeg merge. This is a most peaceful place.

ARKLOW (51m/82km)

Woodenbridge *5m/8km.* Delightful village surrounded by beautiful countryside at the southern end of the Vale of Avoca.

GOREY (61m/98km)

Arts Festival (summer) and Arts Centre, tel. (055) 21470.

Courtown Harbour *3m/5km; infrequent bus.* A popular sea-side resort with sandy dunes.

ENNISCORTHY (79m/126km)

Hillside town above the River Slaney with narrow streets and 1586 castle which is now the country Museum; open summer, Mon-Fri, 10.00-18.00; Sat and Sun all year and Oct-May, Mon, Fri, 14.00-17.30; tel. (054) 3334. Enniscorthy also has a Stawberry Fair in summer, Wexford being famous for its strawberries. **Vinegar Hill** nearby was the chief scene of the fateful 1798 rebellion; worth climbing for views of the Slaney valley. **Carley's Bridge Pottery** fine pottery dating from 1659 and still in production.

From here the railway runs along the Slaney river to Wexford.

WEXFORD (95m/152km)

A 9th-century town with narrow winding streets, quaint old houses and good pubs. The town once had five gates in its walls of which only **Westgate Tower** survives (near station). **Selskar Abbey** (Westgate) is an ancient foundation whose tower is still in use. The first Anglo-Irish treaty was signed here in 1169 and a few years later Henry II of England spent the whole of Lent doing penance for the murder of Thomas Becket. Three years after (1175), Raymond le Gros (the Fat) married the daughter of Strongbow in the abbey.

The **Bullring**, actually used for bull fights at one time, contains a bronze pikeman in memory of the 1798 rebellion which took place mainly in Co. Wexford. Oliver Cromwell stayed at 29 South Main Street while making his sanguinous progress around Ireland, and on Crescent Quay there is a statue of Commodore John Barry (1745-1803), the founder of the US Navy who fought in the American war of independence. Wexford **Maritime Musuem** is aptly

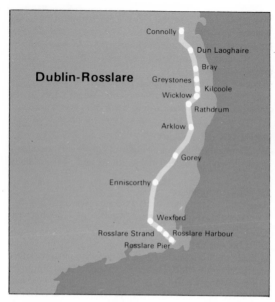

Dublin-Rosslare

Connolly
Dun Laoghaire
Bray
Greystones
Kilcoole
Wicklow
Rathdrum
Arklow
Gorey
Enniscorthy
Wexford
Rosslare Strand   Rosslare Harbour
Rosslare Pier

located in a former lightship moored at the quays and contains items on the town's maritime past and the Irish navy (June-Aug, daily, 10.00-21.00). The **Arts Centre**, Cornmarket, has exhibitions, concerts and drama all year round (Mon-Fri, 10.00-18.00). The world famous **Opera Festival** takes place each October in the Theatre Royal; tickets are in great demand. Lots of fringe arts events are less formal and easier to see (details from TIO). **Mussel Festival** is an annual feast of seafood, talks and exhibitions each September. For traditional **pubs**, try Crown Bar, Skeffington Street, or Kinsella's, Main Street.

Kilmore Quay *10m/16km S; bus from Wexford.* A delightful fishing village with thatched cottages, noted for sea angling. 3m/5km S of Kilmore Quay are the Saltee Islands, each 0.5m/0.8km long comprising a bird sanctuary. Regular boats operate from the quayside in good weather.

Forth Mountain *4m/6km SW; bus from Wexford.* Forest walks and breathtaking views of the whole Wexford coastline from the top.

Tacumshane *12m/19km SE; infrequent bus from Wexford.* Rare example of a 19th-century windmill in full working order. Just west of the town is Lady's Lake. Lady's Island, joined to the mainland by a causeway, has the ruins of a 12th-century castle whose tower has a greater lean than the tower of Pisa.

ROSSLARE STRAND (102m/163km)

Fine 6m/9.5km strand where the railway line from Waterford joins from the right.

ROSSLARE HARBOUR MAINLAND (104m/166km)
ROSSLARE PIER (105m/168km)
The pier is the terminal for car ferries from Le Havre,
Cherbourg, Pembroke and Fishguard and most trains pull
up alongside the main berth.

Dublin-Waterford

---

*4 trains per day; fastest journey 2 hours 20 minutes;
112m/179km*

The line to Waterford passes through rather flat countryside at first before leaving the route to Cork and turning
south to the delightful city of Kilkenny. South of the city
the countryside is rich and fertile. A number of the stations
en route are superb examples of railway architecture, notably Athy, Carlow and Muine Bheag (Bagenalstown); they
have scarcely been altered since they were opened 140
years ago.

HEUSTON STATION (Kingsbridge) *buses 24, 79 from
city centre; bus 90 from Connolly Station.*
For Heuston-Kildare see Dublin-Cork line.
Waterford trains leave the Cork line at Cherryville Junction just past Kildare town.

ATHY (45m/72km)
The Grand Canal joins the navigable River Barrow at
Athy. White's Castle, 16th-century, guards the river cros-
sing in the town while 0.5m/0.8km N is another ruin,

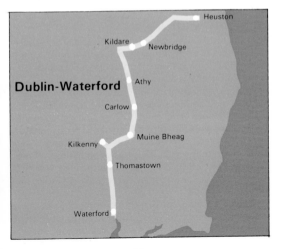

Woodstock Castle, dating from the late 1200s. The modern design of Athy's Dominican Church (1965) features an imposing interior.

CARLOW (56m/90km)

Like Athy, Carlow's substantial castle is located near the Barrow crossing. The large 13th-century structure was at one time much larger until 1814 when a certain Dr Middleton, deciding to turn it into a lunatic asylum, used an over-generous dynamite charge to reduce the walls and managed to destroy half the castle, thereby qualifying himself for admission.

Browne's Hill Dolmen *2m/3km E.* The 100-ton capstone of this very impressive dolmen is the largest in Ireland.

Moone *13m/21km; bus from Carlow via Castledermot.* In the graveyard of this little hamlet is one of the finest high crosses in Ireland, with 51 panels showing many biblical scenes.

MUINE BHEAG (Bagenalstown) (66m/106km)

Named after Walter Bagenal, who set out to build a town of considerable architectural splendour but was unable to complete it. Bagenalstown is nonetheless very pleasantly set on the River Barrow.

Graiguenamanagh *12m/19km S; bus from Bagenalstown.* Very attractive town with a neat arched bridge over the Barrow.

Duiske Abbey, completed in 1240, once covered a good part of the present town. It has been beautifully restored to its original Cistercian simplicity and is now the parish church. Very fine main doorway near the baptistry and original monastic floor tiles. There are lovely walks up and down the river from the town which nestles under Mount Brandon.

KILKENNY (81m/130km)

Beautiful historic city of winding streets and some wonderful buildings of great antiquity; Kilkenny is full of atmosphere. The city was once an important administrative centre and nearly replaced Dublin as the Irish capital at one time. Dating from the 6th century, it was named after a church built by St Canice and was the seat of the Kings of Ossory before being much changed by the Normans. Today is is a bustling, thriving city noted for its sophistication. Kilkenny Arts Week (Aug-Sept) features a wide range of cultural events both formal and fringe all over the city. The county too is known for the high density of potters and craft workers in leather, glass, textiles and metal.

St Canice's Cathedral Starkly beautiful church whose squat tower stands out prominently over the city. Inside there are numerous sculptures and monuments, some as old as 700 years. Although considerably altered over the years, St Canice's is in excellent repair and is one of the finest cathedrals in Ireland. Note the 12th-century St Ciaran's Chair, a simple marble piece with some delightful sculpture on the arms. The nearby round tower gives a splendid view over the whole city.

Kilkenny Castle, The Parade. An outstanding 13th-century castle on a commanding position high above the River Nore. Three sides and three of the original towers give some idea of its original size. The Castle was for many years owned by the Butler family, being the seat of the Marquess of Ormonde. Today it is in state ownership; magnificent views from the splendid apartments over the city. Summer, daily, 10.00-19.00; rest of year, Tues-Sat, 10.00-17.00; Sun, 14.00-17.00.

Kilkenny Design Workshops Opposite the main entrance to the Castle the former stables have been attractively converted to house the Kilkenny Design Workshops, founded by the Irish government to promote good design and quality manufactures. The Workshops feature a display of the best of Irish-made goods which may be purchased here and in the Kilkenny Shop. Nassau Street, Dublin. Mon-Sat, 09.00-18.00

Rothe House, Parliament Street, dates from 1594 and was once the home of Bishop Rothe, a prominent figure in the Confederation of Kilkenny (1642-8) when an independent parliament sat in the city. His very attractive house is now a museum. Note the courtyard well, the outside staircase and the superb craftsmanship of the wooden roofbeams held in place without a single nail or screw.

Black Abbey, Blackmill Street, is a well-restored Dominican church dating from 1225 with some very fine windows.

Black Freren Gate, Abbey Street. The only city gate surviving from the medieval period.

Kyteler's Inn, St Kieran's Street. This is the oldest building in Kilkenny, though heavily restored for modern use as a pub. Dame Alice Kytler, the owner, was a suspected witch and poisoner of four husbands in c. 1324. This formidable lady managed to escape being burnt at the stake (the solution to such problems at the time) but her maid was not so lucky, being executed for complicity in her mistress's crimes.

Walks There are lots of interesting laneways to explore on the west side of Parliament Street and between High Street and St Kieran's Street. Also, delightful riverside walks starting beneath the Castle in either direction.

Dunmore Cave *7m/11km N; bus from Kilkenny*. This is a series of limestone caves and underground chambers with a huge stalagmite pillar known as the market cross. There

Rothe House, Kilkenny

are guided tours of the caves which are well lit and have
viewing galleries. Summer, daily, 11.00-19.15; rest of
year, 11.00-16.00; tel. (056) 27726.

Bennetsbridge *5m/8km SE; bus from Kilkenny.* Charming
village with a lovely old bridge over the Nore. Bennetsbridge is noted for its pottery and other crafts.

THOMASTOWN (92m/147km)

Takes its name from the 13th-century Seneschal of Leinster, Thomas Fitzanthony Walsh, who walled in the town.

Inistioge *5m/8km SE; infrequent bus from Thomastown.*
Delightful village set around a tree-lined square beside
the River Nore which is crossed by a ten-arched bridge.
1m/1.5km S is Woodstock, the former estate of the Tighes,
now an extensive forest park.

Jerpoint Abbey *2m/3km S; infrequent bus from Thomastown.* Soon after leaving the station the train crosses the
Nore by a viaduct with splendid views on either side. The
line then passes close to the stately Jerpoint Abbey on the
right, one of the best kept monastic ruins in the country.
Founded as a Cistercian house in 1190 the chancel has a
fine barrel-vaulted roof; there is also a distinctive square
tower and an impressive cloister with elaborate sculpture
work. Jerpoint is quite beautiful. Summer, daily, 10.00-
19.00; other times by arr. with caretaker's house nearby.

WATERFORD (112m/179km)

Perhaps not the most picturesque city in Ireland, Waterford nonetheless has its charms. Well situated on the
southern bank of the River Suir it was founded by the
Vikings in 853 as Vadrefjord and is today a busy seaport.
The city is best known as the home of Waterford glass,
generally recognised as the finest in the world. An excellent view of the city may be had from Mount Misery on
the north side of the river.

Reginald's Tower, Parade Quay. Built in 1003 by the

Danes this massive circular tower has a conical roof and was for a time used as a prison. Today it houses the Civic Museum with a good collection of artefacts on the city's history.

City Walls Parts of the walls built by the Danes and reinforced by the Normans can be seen close to the station, at Castle Street and Mayor's Walk.

Waterford Glass Factory, Cork Road. Starting in the 1780s and revived after a lapse of some years in 1947, Waterford Glass is treasured all over the world as being without equal. Guided tours of the factory take in all stages of the manufacture. 6 times daily Mon-Fri all year except Aug. Children under 12 not admitted.

Tramore *8m/13km S; bus from Waterford*. Among Ireland's most popular seaside resorts, with a long sandy beach and seaside amusements. Near the town are a number of coastal walks such as that along the Doneraile Cliffs.

New Ross *21m/34km NE; bus from Waterford*. Very old Wexford town on a broad stretch of the River Barrow. The town's steep streets testify to its antiquity. The Tholsel dates from 1749 and has a very pleasant clock tower. There are regular boat trips to Waterford, Inistioge or St Mullins from the quayside, including evening dinner cruises; details from TIO.

Dunganstown *4m/6.4km S; no bus*. The tiny cottage where the grandfather of former US president John F. Kennedy was born has been preserved and is close to the Kennedy Memorial Park, which has a vast selection of trees and plants from all over the world. Lovely views of the surrounding countryside from the many walks. Summer, daily, 10.00-20.00; April and Sept, closes 18.30; Oct-Mar, 17.00; tel. (051) 88171.

Dublin-Cork-Cobh

Dublin-Cork: 9 trains per day; fastest journey 2 hours 35 minutes; 166m/266km
Cork-Cobh: 14 trains per day; journey time 35 minutes; 11m/18km

The Inter-City route to Cork is the busiest in the country, parts of it being used by trains to Galway, Limerick, Tralee, Westport and Waterford. Trains operate at speeds up to 90mph/145kph and the route takes in a good part of the Midlands and Munster. Mileposts are on the left travelling to Cork. The short branch to Cobh is Cork's only suburban rail line and skirts Cork harbour to the former transatlantic port of Cobh.

HEUSTON STATION (Kingsbridge) *buses 24, 79 from city centre; bus 90 from Connelly Station.*

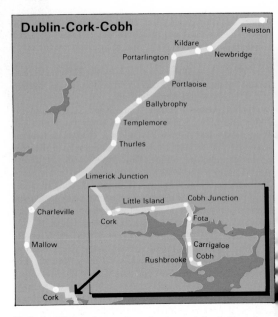

Dublin-Cork-Cobh

Heuston
Kildare
Portarlington
Newbridge
Portlaoise
Ballybrophy
Templemore
Thurles
Limerick Junction
Little Island
Cobh Junction
Charleville
Cork
Fota
Mallow
Carrigaloe
Rushbrooke
Cobh
Cork

Built in 1844 and prominently situated 1m/1.5km from
O'Connell Bridge on the River Liffey, Heuston Station is
a magnificent example of railway architecture, arguably
Ireland's finest. For many years known as Kingsbridge it
is now the headquarters of Córas Iompair Éireann (CIE),
the state company which operates trains and buses in the
Republic. Happily the approach along the quays is unim-
peded and the Renaissance-style façade can be seen from
some distance. So well preserved is it that from time to
time film companies use it to represent Victorian railway
scenes.

Leaving the station, the Phoenix Park can be seen on
the right across the Liffey with the obelisk raised to the
Duke of Wellington.

Inchicore 1.75m/3km out the train passes the mock
Tudor-style engineering works of CIE on the left with its
diamond windows, towers and battlements. Soon after,
the spread of the Dublin Mountains appears on the left
with the cone of Clondalkin round tower visible on the
same side (4.5m/7km).

NEWBRIDGE (Droichead Nua) (26m/42km)

Soon after leaving the station the train begins to cross the
vast, flat pastureland of the Curragh, the heart of the Irish
bloodstock industry, where you'll more than likely see
thoroughbreds being put through their paces. Nearby is
the **Curragh Racecourse** (special trains to the Curragh

Cork city

Station for race meetings, details from CIE) where the
Irish Derby is run each June.

KILDARE (30m/48km)
The town was founded by St Brigid in 490 AD and the
cathedral dedicated to her has many traces of its 750 year
history. Alongside is a 100 ft/30 m round tower of the
same period.

Tully *0.75m/1km S*. The Irish National Stud, the premier
horse breeding centre, is located at Tully and includes a
Horse Museum. The picturesque **Japanese Gardens** are
located in the grounds and feature a floral representation
of the stages of a person's life (Easter-Oct, Mon-Sat, 10.30-
17.30; Sun, 14.00-17.30; tel. (045) 21251).

Monasterevin *6m/9.5km SW; bus from Kildare*. An attractive village on the Grand Canal with an unusual swivel
bridge and acqueduct carrying the canal over the River
Barrow; these can be seen from the train on the left at
milepost 36.75/59km, although the train does not stop
here; peaceful canal walks from the town.

Moore Abbey (18th-century) just outside the town, now
a hospital, was once the home of the celebrated Irish tenor
John McCormack.

PORTARLINGTON (42m/67km)
Very fine station building of the Great Southern and West-

ern Railway; even the water tower on the left is incorporated into the overall design. Portarlington was founded by Huguenot refugees who came from France in the 17th century and built many of the tall houses and elaborate gardens to be seen in the town. The French Church off the main square has a continental air and each September French Week features an historical pageant and novelties such as a snail-eating contest. It is also the location of Ireland's first turf-burning electricity generating station.

The Galway/Westport line branches to the right outside the station.

PORTLAOISE (51m/82km)
Rock of Dunamase *3m/5km E; no bus*. This ancient fortress mentioned by the Greek cartographer Ptolemy became the castle of the kings of Leinster and is now a magnificent ruin dominating the countryside for miles.

Between here and Ballybrophy the Slieve Bloom Mountains dominate the landscape on the right hand side with their heavy forestry plantation.

Abbeyleix *9m/14.5km S; bus from Portlaoise*. Very attractive tree-lined main street in the town which gets its name from a 12th-century abbey of which nothing remains. **Abbeyleix House** dates from 1773 and is the de Vesci home (private). The superb gardens are worth seeing (Easter-Sept, 14.30-18.30). North of the town is the site of the 1599 battle between Owen MacRory O'More and the Earl of Essex which ended the latter's Irish campaign. The place is known as the Pass of the Plumes from the number of plumed helmets left on the field afterwards.

BALLYBROPHY (67m/107km)
Change here for Limerick via Roscrea and Nenagh; 2 trains daily.

TEMPLEMORE (79m/127km)
The training centre for the Garda Siochana, the national police force, is located in Templemore. The town is close to the remarkable Devil's Bit Mountain (visible on the right) which has a prominent gap at its peak. The legend is that the Devil took a chunk of it one day but finding it indigestible spat it out violently and where it landed was formed the Rock of Cashel.

THURLES (87m/139km)
Cashel *13m/21km S; bus from Thurles*. Delightful town in the centre of a plain dominated by the magnificent Rock of Cashel (200ft/60m) which is visible for miles around. For 700 years, until 1101, it was the palace of the Kings of Munster. The royal household here was converted by St Patrick in 450, and 500 years later Brian Boru was crowned King of Munster at Cashel. The Rock was for many years an important ecclesiastical centre.

The Cathedral is the largest building on the Rock. Now roofless, it is cruciform in shape and contains numerous monuments to archbishops of Cashel. An excellent way to view it is by climbing the 127 steps to the narrow high level walkway which runs almost all the way round (not for those afraid of heights).

Cormac's Chapel This impressive church was built in 1134 by Cormac MacCarthy and has two unusual square towers on either side of the barrel vaulted roof. The present entrance has some noteworthy carvings around the doorway which are continued in the rather dark interior; worth bringing a torch.

The nearby round tower is in excellent repair and 92 ft/28 m high. The splendid Bishop's Palace in the town is now a hotel and has a rather taxing pathway leading directly up to the Rock.

LIMERICK JUNCTION (107m/172km)
Change here for Limerick, Tipperary town, Clonmel and Carrick-on-Suir. This busy junction was once a famous railway oddity on account of its eccentric layout which required that *every* train had to reverse at least once and some up to three times.

CHARLEVILLE (Rathluirc) (129m/206km)

MALLOW (145m/232km)
Situated on the river Blackwater, Mallow has a number of elegant 18th-century houses and was once noted for its medicinal spa waters. Mallow Castle (1584) has many original features and the museum is open all year round each afternoon.

The station is now the base for the Great Southern Railway Preservation Society, whose vintage rolling stock can be seen in the process of restoration.

Anne's Grove Gardens *6m/9.5km E; bus from Mallow.* Elaborate gardens in a delightful riverside setting (mid Apr-Sept, Sun-Fri, 13.00-17.00; tel. (022) 26145.

Fermoy *21m/34km E; bus from Mallow.* Very attractive town on the River Blackwater (noted for trout, salmon and coarse fishing) with elegant trees lining both banks. There are many lovely walks around Fermoy, among them Barnane Walk with views of Castlehyde House, home of Douglas Hyde, the first President of Ireland. Another delightful stroll starts at the mill and continues along the right bank of the river to Carrigabrick railway bridge and thence to the old castle.

CORK (166m/266km)
The second city in the Republic, the Munster capital is set on the River Lee whose two channels divide Cork and are crossed by numerous bridges. It is a busy commercial centre and port with its own strong individuality. Recently

Cork celebrated its 800th aniversary — and there is a lot to celebrate.

Cathedrals and churches: Shandon Church, Shandon Street, dominates the northside with its pepperpot steeple dating from 1722. Two sides are of red sandstone, the others of grey, and the tower gives excellent views of the whole city. Best of all you can practise ringing the famous Shandon Bells. **St Finbarre's Cathedral**, South Mall, is a sizeable 100-year-old Gothic style building with interesting mosaics. On display is a cannon ball fired during the 1690 siege of the city.

Public Buildings: City Hall, Albert Quay: Cork's municipal centre has an impressive marble vestibule and main staircase with a large assembly/concert room upstairs (daily, 09.00-17.00). **Cork Museum**, Fitzgerald's Park (3, 7, 7A buses from Patrick Street; Mon-Fri, 11.00-17.00, Sat and Sun, 11.00-13.00. The City Museum has a wide display of items on Cork from prehistoric times to the recent past. **Crawford Municipal School of Art**, Emmet Place (Mon-Sat, 10.00-17.30; Sun, 14.00-18.00). Contains a good collection of mainly Irish art, painting and sculpture. **Court House**, Washington Street: this 1835 building has a broad Corinthian portico raised above street level and superimposed by statues of Justice, Law and Mercy. The façade on Liberty Street is in Tudor style (Mon-Fri, 19.00-17.00).

Entertainment: Opera House, Emmet Place, for frequent concerts and plays; tel, (021) 20022/23680. **Everyman Playhouse**, Fr Mathew Street, has regular theatrical performances from local and invited groups; tel. (021) 26287. **Granary Theatre**, University College (no. 5 bus from Patrick Street) has a variety of plays, etc. during term time; tel. (021) 26871. **Cork School of Music**, Union Quay, lunchtime and evening concerts through the year; tel. (021) 20076. **Entertainment Centre**, Grand Parade, summertime traditional shows (details from TIO, tel. (021) 23251).

Pubs and markets: for traditional pubs try Le Chateau (1793), Patrick Street; Teach Beag, Oliver Plunkett Street for Irish music; Dan Lowry's, MacCurtain Street, antique furniture and stained glass; the Vineyard, Market Lane for rugby fans. The Antiques Market, 7 Tuckey Street, is open Friday and Saturday, 10.30-17.30, and at Coal Quay there is a lively fruit and vegetable market.

Walks: Patrick Street and Grand Parade are Cork's main thoroughfares for shopping and sightseeing and run between the two main channels of the Lee. South Mall is the business centre. Climb **Patrick's Hill**, steep but worth it for the panorama of the whole city. **Marina** is a pleasant riverside walk to Blackrock Castle (2m/3km). **Ballincollig**

Kinsale, Co. Cork
5m/8km W; bus from Parnell Place. Gentle walk along the river from Powder Mills.

Around Cork:

Blarney *5m/8km NW; bus from Parnell Place.* The 15th-century castle is famous for the Blarney Stone which imparts eloquence on those who kiss it; lovely approach through parkland and views from the battlements, (all year, daily, 09.30-dusk).

Crosshaven *17m/27km SE; bus from Parnell Place.* Seaside resort and a popular yachting centre much frequented by Corkonians.

Kinsale *18m/29km S; bus from Parnell Place.* Lovely old world town noted for its numerous first class restaurants (Gourmet Festival Oct. details TIO). Kinsale has strong Spanish connections going back 400 years which have left their mark in its winding streets and unusual architecture. **Museum**, Old Town Hall, has lots of maritime exhibits and memorabilia of the Lusitania sunk off the Old Head of Kinsale in 1917. **St Multose Church** (1179) has a very fine interior, including the town stocks for punishing malefactors.

A delightful way to view Kinsale and the Bandon Estuary is to take the circular walk around Compass Hill (2m/3km, signposted) which starts above the Trident Hotel. Another walk is through the fishermen's quarter, the Scilly, to Summer Cove and **Charles Fort**, a prominent ruin of a 1677 fortress which was occupied by the military until 1922 and now has echoing buildings and creepy dungeons.

Cork-Cobh

The Cork suburban rail line is an interesting excursion around the islands of Cork harbour which crosses three viaducts en route. Note the superb 1848 steam engine of the Great Southern and Western Railway on display in the station concourse.

CORK
See above

LITTLE ISLAND (4m/7km)
COBH JUNCTION
The branch to Youghal, once a destination for Sunday seaside trains but now closed, leaves here on the left. **Midleton** (*7m/11km E; bus from Cobh Junction*) is the main distillery for Irish whiskey where you can see how it is made and taste a sample. To visit, tel. (021) 631821.

FOTA (6m/11km)
The spectacularly beautiful **Fota House** has recently been restored at great expense and is now open to the public. It contains a fine collection of period furniture and works of art. A large part of the grounds has been converted into a zoo and is open daily, Easter-Oct, 14.30-17.30 (check times with TIO).

CARRIGALOE (8m/14km)
RUSHBROOKE (10m/17km)
COBH (11m/18km)
Once a major naval base and embarkation point for trans-atlantic liners and emigrant ships, Cobh is set on a commanding position overlooking Cork Harbour. It is the home of the Royal Cork Yacht Club (founded 1720), the oldest such club in the world. Haulbowline Island, south of the town, is today the headquarters of the Irish Naval Service and there are regular trips around the harbour in summer. **St Colman's Cathedral** with its slender spire dominates the town and is noted for its flying buttresses, rose windows, mosaic flooring, carved pillars and peal of 47 bells.

West Cork

The area of Cork west of the city has some of the loveliest countryside in Ireland. Although once served by a wide rail network, today bus services have replaced the trains. A number of routes are operated from Cork City. One of the most scenic is the summer only Expressway service which runs from Cork to Killarney via Bandon, Clonakilty, Rosscarbery, Skibbereen, Bantry, Glengarriff and Kenmare. This bus stops only at the places listed below and the time for the 125m/200km journey is about 5 hours.

BANDON (20m/32km)

A 17th-century town with some fragments of the old town walls. Killrogan Church dates from 1710 and has the town stocks.

CLONAKILTY (34m/55km)

A major agricultural centre with a superb beach at Inchadoney (3m/5km). Michael Collins (1890-1922), the leader in the War of Independence, was born at Woodfield, outside Clonakilty. There is a West Cork Festival centred on the town each June/July.

ROSCARBERY (42m/67km)

The ancient cathedral of Roscarbery, founded in the 6th century, has been restored and is now the principal item of interest in the town.

LEAP (48m/77km)

1.5m/2.5km S of Leap is the pretty fishing village of Glandore in an idyllic harbour setting. The area is noted for its mild, sub-tropical climate.

SKIBBEREEN (55m/88km)

5m/8km SE (no bus) is the unusual village of Castletownsend, whose narrow street running down to the harbour is divided midway by a tree. This was the home of Edith Somerville and Violet Martin, authors of *Reminiscences of an Irish RM* among other works. The nearby church has some excellent Harry Clarke windows and an array of monuments to prominent military and naval figures once associated with the town.

BANTRY (76m/122km)

Spectacularly situated, Bantry nestles on the shores of the famous bay and is a good base for exploring other parts of West Cork. **Bantry House** (mid 18th-century) has a fine collection of art treasures, paintings, tapestries and sculptures. Daily, 09.00-18.00; summer till 20.00.

GLENGARRIFF (87m/139km)

Very popular tourist resort, famous for its Mediterranean climate which produces luxuriant flowers, shrubs and trees. Garinish Island (frequent boats all year from Blue Pool) has famous Italian and Japanese gardens, shrubberies, nature walks and many rare tropical plants.

KENMARE (104m/166km)

Here the road joins the Ring of Kerry (*see Dublin-Killarney-Tralee line*). The Expressway bus makes its final stop at Killarney Railway Station (125m/200km).

Dublin-Killarney-Tralee

4 trains per day; fastest journey 3 hours 35 minutes; 207m/331km

Dublin-Tralee is the longest passenger train run in Ireland. Following the Cork route as far as Mallow, the line swings west at Killarney Junction after crossing the Blackwater Viaduct and runs through lovely mountainous countryside to the popular tourist resort of Killarney, terminating at Tralee.

The station buildings between Mallow and Killarney are solid little structures, aften with a pair of attractive cottages set back from the line.

See Dublin-Cork chapter for the line between Heuston and Mallow.

Ladies View, Killarney

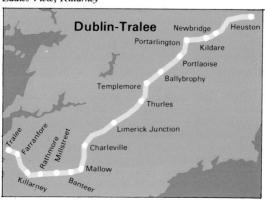

Dublin-Tralee

Heuston
Newbridge
Portarlington
Kildare
Portlaoise
Ballybrophy
Templemore
Thurles
Limerick Junction
Charleville
Mallow
Banteer
Millstreet
Rathmore
Farranfore
Tralee
Killarney

KILLARNEY JUNCTION (146m/234km)

BANTEER (157m/251km)

For an excellent view of the Blackwater valley, climb Mount Hillary, 2m/3km SE of Banteer.

McDonough's Folly *4m/6.5km N; bus from Banteer.* This massive castle begun in the 1500s was never completed. The authorities took fright at the notion of such an impregnable fortress and ordered construction work to cease.

MILLSTREET (165m/264km)

Home of the prestigious annual Horse Show which attracts a worldwide entry.

RATHMORE (171m/274km)

KILLARNEY (186m/298km)

Ireland's world famous beauty spot and premier tourist attraction, whose mountains and lakes have assumed an almost magical aura.

Approaching the town the train runs alongside the delightful River Flesk for several miles. The chief item of interest in Killarney town is **St Mary's Cathedral**, designed by A. W. Pugin in 1842.

Lakes of Killarney

The **Lakes of Killarney** can be visited on foot, by bicycle, hired car, organised tour or jaunting car. Check at the TIO for tour rates and times.

Half-day tour; 12m/19km Heading south from the town the road runs along the shoreline of the pretty Lower Lake to pass near the extensive 15th-century ruin of Muckross Abbey. Staircases lead from the beautiful tree-shaded cloister to the upper floor of the monastery which contains the dormitory, refectory, infirmary and scriptorium. Muckross House nearby is a fine 1843 mansion presented with Muckross Estate to the Irish nation in 1932. It now holds the fascinating Kerry Folk Museum, while in the house itself you can see potters, carpenters, weavers and blacksmiths at work. The gardens are a delight, with lovely mountain views on all sides. Open Mar-June and Sept-Oct daily, 10.00-19.00; July-Aug daily, 9.00-21.00; Nov-Feb, Tues-Sun, 10.00-19.00.

The road continues around the lake, crossing the Muckross Peninsula by Brickeen Bridge near to pretty Dinis Island. The path near Dinis Cottage gives superb views of the Meeting of the Waters and the Old Weir Bridge. Torc Waterfall is passed on the right and a delightful pathway runs along it up through the woods to an excellent spot for viewing the lakes and Torc Mountain. The route back to Killarney is then via the main road.

Full-day tour; 25m/40km Leaving Killarney via New Street, turn left to cross the River Laune within sight of Dunloe Castle. Straight ahead is the spectacular Gap of Dunloe, a narrow mountain pass 4m/6.5km long which can be traversed on foot or by pony and trap (vehicles not admitted). At the entrance is Kate Kearney's Cottage, now a souvenir shop. Rushing streams and huge rock formations are evident in the defile whose narrow sides have a remarkable echo. At the head of the Gap the Upper Lake is visible in the valley 3m/5km away.

This lake is crossed by boat through the straits known as the Long Range beneath the Eagle's Nest on the left. Then, slipping under the Old Weir Bridge to the Meeting of the Waters, the boat crosses Muckross Lake to the Lower Lake, passing dozens of islands on the way. Boats moor at Ross Castle, 2m/3km from Killarney town centre.

Around Killarney:
Ladies' View *12m/19km SW; bus from Killarney.* This famous viewing point over the lakes acquired its name after Queen Victoria expressed her delight at the prospect.
Innisfallen *1m/1.5km from Ross Castle by boat.* In the very ancient monastery on this beautiful island monks compiled the *Annals of Innisfallen*, a record of world events between 950 and 1320. The Annals are now in the Bodleian Library, Oxford.
Killarney National Park *3m/5km S; bus from Killarney.* Marvellously wild parkland of 20,000 acres with wild deer and a herd of pedigree Kerry cows.
Ring of Kerry
This very popular excursion around the Waterville Peninsula takes in some of the finest scenery in Ireland and is best made by tourist coach or car as parts are not served by the regular service bus. The round trip is 110m/176km.
Kenmare Heading south past Muckross Lake and the Upper Lake the road runs through magnificent mountain scenery descending to the picturesque town of Kenmare, noted for its gourmet Seafood Festival, Sept/Oct. Turning west the shoreline has splendid views of the mountains across the bay. Sneem is a pretty village of bright colours set around a fair green. 2m/3km NE is **Staigue Fort**, the finest example of an ancient fortress in Ireland. In almost

The Skelligs, Co. Kerry

perfect condition, the circular fortress consists of a dry
stone wall with several flights of steps leading to the top;
well worth a diversion. There are very fine views between
here and Waterville.

Caherdaniel 1m/1.5km S of the town is **Derrynane
House**, the former home of the patriot Daniel O'Connell.
The house is now a museum and displays the furniture
and personal effects of O'Connell. The adjacent park has
lovely walks and sea views. Summer, daily, 10.00-19.00;
rest of year, Tues-Sat, 10.00-13.00: Sun, 14.00-17.00.
Waterville, on the shore of Ballinskelligs Bay, is known
as an angling centre and has some excellent beaches to the
NW of the town. To the east is the idyllic Lough Currane.
Caherciveen is the birthplace of Daniel O'Connell and
the embarkation point for nearby **Valentia Island** which

is linked to the mainland by a bridge at Portmagee. Boats can also be taken from Cahirciveen to the Skelligs, two extraordinary uninhabited islands rising like mountain pinnacles from the sea. Landing can be difficult in all but the calmest weather at **Skellig Michael** but the effort, involving a steep climb of 500 steps up the cliff face, is well worth it. Clinging to the rock are the remains of an ancient Christian monastery, a church, beehive huts, and oratories. Skellig Michael is truly remarkable. Little Skellig is home to 20,000 gannets and normally inaccessible.

From Cahirciveen to Glenbeigh the scenery is beautifully varied, and climbing to Kells there are superb views across Dingle Bay. There is also a delightful walk known as the Glenbeigh Horseshoe around the hills near the town from Seefin to Drung Hill.

The next town on the Ring of Kerry, Killorglin, is famous for its **Puck Fair**, three days and nights of revelry in August when the star is a buck goat which is enthroned amid great ceremony as King Puck.

The last stretch of the Ring of Kerry follows the Laune River to Killarney.

Killarney Station being built as a terminus the train first reverses before turning north away from the town, with views of Magillicuddy's Reeks on the left.

FARRANFORE (196m/314km)
Plane trips from Farranfore Airport for viewing Kerry from the air.

TRALEE (207m/331km)
The county town of Kerry is a busy commercial and tourist centre and an excellent base for exploring the Dingle Peninsula. The **Rose of Tralee Festival** attracts comely contestants from all over the world in Aug/Sept and the crack goes on for more than a week. The **Siamsa Tíre Theatre**, Staughton's Row, works hard at preserving true Irish folk theatre in several centres and has regular summer performances; details from the TIO or tel. (066) 23055.

Around Tralee:
Dingle Peninsula For many years up to the 1950s a spectacular and rather dangerous steam train made its leisurely way across the mountains between Dingle and Tralee. It was by all accounts infinitely more exciting than the prosaic bus which follows the same route today. Nonetheless the scenery by road is lovely.

Two bus routes are available; the one via Camp is the more interesting and has lovely views of the whole peninsula. The more southern route through Castlemaine passes the vast, golden Inch Strand which featured in the film *Ryan's Daughter*.

Almost completely surrounded by hills, Dingle is a lovely old town in the Kerry Gaeltacht with good pubs, shops and restaurants noted for freshly caught fish.

The bus service west of Dingle is infrequent, but runs 2-3 days per week to Ventry, Ballyferriter and Dunquin. From the inimitable Kruger Kavanagh's pub in Ventry at the far end of Europe you can gaze out on the Atlantic and the **Blasket Islands** which produced such famous writers as Peig Sayers and Tomás Ó Crohan. Boat trips to the islands from Dunquin.

Gallarus Oratory *(2m/3km NE of Ballyferriter)* is a perfectly preserved 8th-century church whose arched roof and dry stone walls have resisted rain and wind for over 1,000 years. Note also the many hundreds of beehive huts to be seen on the hillsides between Inch and Dunquin.

Slea Head *(2m/3km S of Dunquin)* has a superb panorama

out to sea and some very fine beaches on which you may well see *currachs*, traditional fishing craft.

Dublin-Limerick (via Roscrea)

1 train per day; fastest journey 2 hour 10 minutes; 123m/ 197km; the main Dublin-Limerick service is via Limerick Junction (9 trains per day).

The branch line to Limerick via Roscrea provides connections off the Cork main line at Ballybrophy. The terrain is rather flat for the most part until the Silvermines Mountains come into view on the left soon after Nenagh and the Shannon is glimpsed briefly near Birdhill.

At Killonan, 4.5m/7km E of Limerick, the line joins that from Tipperary and Limerick Junction.

See Dublin-Cork chapter for the line between Heuston and Ballybrophy.

BALLYBROPHY (67m/107km)

ROSCREA (77m/123km)

Roscrea Castle in the centre of the town was built in 1281 and is guarded by a series of gate towers. Inside the castle grounds is the magnificent 250-year-old **Damer House**, recently saved from destruction and now lovingly restored with its beautiful staircase and interior decor. The **Roscrea Heritage Centre** is now located here and has an excellent collection of rural furniture, among the best in the country, as well as examples of craftwork and domestic utensils. Open July and Aug, Thurs-Mon, 11.00-18.00; Easter-June and Sept, Thurs-Mon, 14.00-18.00; tel. (0505) 21850.

Cistercian College *3m/5km W; bus from Roscrea*. This modern abbey on extensive farmland is a boarding school and has an unusual folklore and natural history museum. By arr., tel. (0505) 21711.

Birr *12m/19km N; bus from Roscrea*. A very pleasant town attractively laid out with some very fine Georgian houses; **Birr Castle** was built in 1627 by Sir Laurence Parsons (Birr was once called Parsonstown) and became in time the seat of the Earls of Rosse. The family was noted for scientific achievement, and the third earl built the famous Rosse astronomical telescope in the mid-19th century. For 80 years this was the largest telescope in the world and attracted many astronomers to Birr. The small museum has an display of items associated with the telescope. Also worth viewing are the castle gardens which produce a splendid colourful display in summer. All year, daily, 09.00-18.00 or dusk.

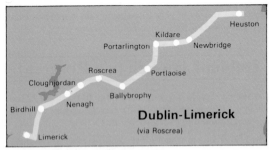

CLOUGHJORDAN (87m/139km)

NENAGH (97m/155km)

Nenagh is the principal town in the thriving agricultural region of north Tipperary. The surviving keep of **Nenagh**

King John's Castle, Limerick

Castle built in the 13th century is among the best preserved in the country and was part of the curtain walls.

BIRDHILL (110m/176km)
Killaloe *5m/8km N; bus from Birdhill.* Delightful little town on the River Shannon below Lough Derg which is a centre for cruiser hire. The **Cathedral of St Flannan** dates from 1182 and is an attractive building whose chief item of interest is the highly ornamented south doorway.

For a scenic view of Lough Derg, other than by boat, take the bus from Killaloe to Tuamgraney and Scariff (11m/17.5km). The road passes near the fort of Beal Boru, from which Brian Boru took his name. Nearby is the site of his palace, Kincora. Scariff is situated on one of the loveliest parts of the lough.

LIMERICK (123m/197km)
Ireland's fourth city is situated on the River Shannon and has three historical sectors: Irish Town, English Town

and Newtown Pery. The latter was built by Edmund Pery (1719-1806), Speaker of the Irish House of Commons, and has a number of fine Georgian streets and squares. The original settlement of the city was made by the Vikings who were in time displaced by Brian Boru.

King John's Castle, Thomond Bridge. Built in the 13th century, the massive walls and towers provide a fine view of the city and the river and still show the scars of the 1690 and 1691 sieges. At the end of Thomond Bridge is the **Treaty Stone** on which Patrick Sarsfield signed the surrender of the city to the Williamite General Winkel in 1691. Sarsfield led the garrison out of the city and 11,000 soldiers went into exile to fight in the French and Spanish armies.

City Walls There are few traces of the walls which once encircled the city but substantial remains can be found in Lelia Street.

St Mary's Cathedral, Nicolas Street, was founded in 1172 by Donal O'Brien, King of Munster, but has been greatly altered. Among the items of interest are the 500-year-old intricately carved black oak misericords. These were upright seat supports for use by monks who were not allowed to sit during the lengthy choral office, and take their name from the Latin word for mercy *misericordia*.

Limerick Museum, St John's Square, has an unusual collection of items on Limerick's history; well laid out and very enjoyable; Mon-Fri, 10.00-17.00.

Belltable Arts Centre, 69 O'Connell Street. This is a thriving arts and cultural centre with theatre, shows and exhibitions.

The Granary, Michael Street. Ingenious conversion of an 18th-century warehouse for use as a crafts centre with its own pub, restaurant and entertainment.

National Institute for Higher Education, Plassey. The Institute holds the fascinating Hunt Collection of early and pre-Christian Irish and European antiquities; well worth a visit. Mon-Fri, 09.30-17.30.

Around Limerick:

Bunratty Castle and Folk Park *8m/13km W; bus from Limerick*. The solid 15th century Bunratty Castle was the fortress of the Earls of Thomond and has been carefully restored to its medieval splendour. The Castle contains an unequalled collection of Irish furniture and tapestries. Ask to see the murder hole over the maingate. Medieval banquets take place in the Banqueting Hall all year round; details TIO or tel. (061) 61511.

The **Folk Park** beside the Castle has a unique collection of Irish cottages and houses taken from all over the country and re-erected here. Each one represents a different rural livelihood: fishing, farming, basket weaving, bread making, farriery, etc, and contains original furniture and ornaments. Castle open daily, 09.30-17.00; Folk Park open till 20.00 in summer.

Durty Nelly's Highly characteristic pub beside the castle with open fires, rural hand tools, furniture and good food; reputed never to close.

Adare *10m/16km SW; bus from Limerick.* Exquisite, old fashioned village of thatched cottages and leafy lanes which is maintained in immaculate condition. Adare Manor is an unusual 18th-century mansion, substantially rebuilt in the last century. It was the home of the Earls of Dunraven until being sold.

Among the monastic ruins in the town the best preserved is that of the Franciscan Friary founded by the Earl of Kildare in 1464 and pleasantly sited beside the river. Still standing are a tower, two chapels and the cloisters. Other monastic sites are the Trinitarian Abbey and the Augustinian Abbey. Desmond Castle also overlooks the river and the extensive ruins consist of a moat surrounding a large inner courtyard.

Craggaunowen Project *14m/22.5km NW; bus from Limerick.* This is a remarkable reconstuction of a bronze age lake dwelling or *crannóg* and a ring fort. They give a vivid impression of daily life in ancient Ireland. The 16th-century castle close by has a comprehensive collection of Irish and continental furniture as well as old rural artifacts; daily, 09.30-17.30.

Knappogue Castle *13m/21km NW; bus from Limerick.* Nearby is the castle dating from 1467 which has been completely restored and now hosts medieval banquets. Details from TIO or tel. (061) 71103.

Rathkeale *18m/29km SW; bus from Limerick.* The 15th-century Castle Matrix is built on the site of a shrine to the pagan goddess Matrix and has been recently restored. Inside the castle where the Elizabethan poet Edmund Spenser met the adventurer Walter Raleigh is the library, which has a very fine collection of first editions. Tours of the castle and grounds summer, Tues-Sat, 14.00-16.30; tel. (061) 64284.

Limerick-Rosslare

2 trains per day (1 only Limerick Junction-Waterford, Sept-May); fastest journey 3 hours 35 minutes; 115m/184km

This is one of the few surviving cross country lines and is worth travelling despite infrequent service as it is a very

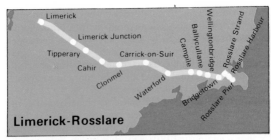

Limerick-Rosslare

scenic route through the mountainous south Tipperary region to the port of Waterford and then through Co. Wexford to terminate at Rosslare Pier.

LIMERICK
See Dublin-Limerick chapter

LIMERICK JUNCTION (22m/35km)
See Dublin-Cork line. The quaint layout still requires that trains to and from Tipperary must make one reversal at 'the Junction'.

TIPPERARY (25m/40km)
Set in the heart of the Golden Vale, Tipperary is an important dairy farming centre and was the birthplace of James O'Neill, father of the American dramatist Eugene O'Neill.

From here the Galtee Mountains are visible on the right and between them and the Slievenamuck Hills is the beauty spot of the Glen of Aherlow whose gentle slopes were once the scene of many battles in pre-Christian times and became a refuge for insurgents 200 years ago.

CAHIR (39m/62km)
The principal sight here is the superb **Cahir Castle**, built in 1142 by Conor O'Brien to guard the Suir crossing and still lived in today. Note in particular the vast courtyard, keep and massive walls. Open summer, daily, 10.00-19.00; rest of year, Tues-Sat, 10.00-17.00; Sun, 14.00-17.00. **Cahir Park**, south of the town, runs along the river and gives pleasant views. Also nearby are the ruins of the 13th-century **Cahir Abbey**. The town has a number of well--preserved Georgian houses.

CLONMEL (50m/80km)
Approaching Cluain Meala, the Honey Meadow, the River Suir and the Comeragh Mountains come into view on the right and the railway runs along the Suir Valley until well past Carrick-on-Suir. Clonmel has a lovely riverside setting with attractive walks near the town. The West Gate arches over the Main Street and parts of the original town walls may be seen near St Mary's church, which has a lovely interior. **Museum and Art Gallery**, Parnell Street, has a collection of items relating to Tipperary's history.

Glen of Aherlow, Co. Tipperary

Soon after leaving the station Slievenamon Mountain, celebrated in the song of that name, comes into view on the left.

CARRICK-ON-SUIR (63m/101km)

This beautiful town on a delightful stretch of river has two parts connected by a pair of bridges. On the south side Carrickbeg is set on a steep hill with the magnificent **Carrick Castle** nearby. This Elizabethan fortress is unique of its kind in Ireland and was built in the 16th century for the Butler family, the Earls of Ormonde. Some claim that Anne Boleyn, the second of Henry VIII's transitory wives, was born in Carrick Castle. Among the original parts of the house is the magnificent fireplace. Opening hours from TIO.

WATERFORD (77m/123km)

See Dublin-Waterford line. Heading east the train runs along the shoreline of Waterford Harbour for several miles with lovely views on the right before coming to the Barrow Bridge. At 2,131 ft/650 m it is the longest railway bridge in Ireland, with an opening central span for ships heading up the Barrow to New Ross; delightful panorama of the estuary.

CAMPILE (86m/138km)

Dunbrody Abbey is an attractive Cistercian abbey near the town; it was built in the 13th century by a follower of Strongbow and occupied by monks of St Mary's Abbey, Dublin. Note the small chapels, windows and the 15th-century tower. The abbot of the monastery held a seat in the Irish Parliament, the last encumbent being Alexander Devereux, the Bishop of Ferns in 1537.

Ballyhack *3m/5km S; no bus.* Very pleasant fishing village with a ferry service to Passage East across the river. The latter is a pleasant spot with splendid views from the nearby hill. The ruined castle in Passage East was once the property of the Knights Templar, an immensely powerful semi-monastic military order which was prominent in the middle ages.

Tintern Abbey *8m/13km SE; bus from Campile.* This monastery was founded in 1200 by William the Marshall in thanksgiving for surviving a shipwreck on the nearby coast. He brought monks from the Welsh abbey of the same name.

BALLYCULLANE (90m/144km)

WELLINGTONBRIDGE (94m/150km)

There was once a major Viking settlement here but no trace remains.

BRIDGETOWN (104m/166km)

ROSSLARE STRAND (112m/179km)

At this point the line joins that from Dublin to Rosslare Pier.

See also Dublin-Rosslare chapter.

Dublin-Galway

5 trains per day; fastest journey 2 hours 25 minutes; 129m/206km

The service to Galway was opened by the Midland Great Western Railway in 1851. Originally it ran from the Broadstone Station, Dublin (now a CIE garage) via Mullingar. Some years ago the terminal changed to Heuston Station and trains now run via Portarlington, crossing the Shannon at Athlone to terminate at Galway, the City of the Tribes. The city is a perfect base for exploring the West of Ireland.

HEUSTON STATION (Kingsbridge) *buses 24, 79 from city centre; bus 90 from Connolly Station.*
For Heuston-Portarlington see Dublin-Cork line.

TULLAMORE (58m/93km)

An agricultural and distilling centre (Irish Mist Liqueur is made here) which grew up as a result of the Grand Canal's prosperity. Leaving the station the line crosses the canal with its neat towpath (for horse-drawn barges) which is ideal for walks; note the solid medieval castle next to the waterway. Holiday cruisers can be hired in the town and there are a number of large buildings associated with the boom days of the Canal.

CLARA (65m/104km)

ATHLONE (81m/130km)

Athlone is strategically placed on the River Shannon between the provinces of Leinster and Connacht. It is now a road and rail junction as well as a busy harbour for Shannon cruising. During the many invasions of Ireland Athlone was the scene of numerous battles and sieges, being one of the principal approaches to Connacht.

King John's Castle (13th-century) is in good repair, with a museum and the governor's apartments. The high curtain wall has a number of loopholes which provide good views over the town and the river.

Auburn *11m/17.5km NW; bus from Athlone.* This is the site of Goldsmith's home, 'Sweet Auburn' or Lissoy which is intimately described in 'The Deserted Village'.

Clonmacnoise *12m/19km S; no bus.* The best way to approach the great monastic settlement of Clonmacnoise is by water. (If you see a boat heading south for Athlone, ask for a lift!) Seen from the Shannon, its towers and crosses seem to rise out of the twisting river. Founded by St Ciaran in 548, Clonmacnoise grew to be one of the leading university cities in Europe, lasting for over 1,000 years. Although frequently raided and burned by invader and native alike, the ruins today are quite substantial and consist of a cathedral, eight churches, two round towers, several high crosses, a castle and 200 beautifully ornamented stone slabs dating from the 6th-11th century, a number of which are mounted near the entrance from the roadway. The **Cross of the Scriptures** stands in front of the cathedral and is eleborately engraved on all sides with biblical scenes. It was made for the grave of King Flann, who died in 914. A short walk away is the **Nun's Church**, dating from the 10th century. Its great west doorway is a beautiful piece of Romanesque work. Clonmacnoise has always been a centre of pilgrimage and the tradition survives on the Sunday nearest 9 September.

Lough Ree To the north of Athlone is Lough Ree, 15m/24km long and 1-6m/1.5-9.5km wide. The lake is peppered with islands, many with remains of ancient churches such as Hare Island, Inchbofin and Saints Island. Boats

Clonmacnoise, Co. Offaly

can be hired in Athlone to explore the Shannon north and south of the town; details, TIO.

Immediately after leaving the station the train crosses the river with fine views of the town, the weir and the castle on the left.

BALLINASLOE (94m/150km)
Aughrim *6m/9.5km SW; bus from Ballinasloe.* The scene of a 1691 battle between Williamites and Jacobites which was of greater significance than the Battle of the Boyne. The museum in St Catherine's school has a large number of mementos of the battle as well as domestic utensils from the period. Tel. (091) 3717.

WOODLAWN (104m/166km)

Dublin-Galway

ATTYMON (110m/176km)

Once the junction for the branch line in Loughrea (*see below*). The line closed in 1975 but is being restored by the West of Ireland Railway Society as a pleasure ride.

ATHENRY (116m/186km)

This town has the best preserved Norman walls in the country, with 5 of the 6 towers still standing.

Loughrea 12m/19km SE; bus from Athenry. The plain

exterior of **St Brendan's Cathedral** conceals a magnificent collection of stained glass windows by Sarah Purser, Evie Hone and others. The church museum contains many examples of contemporary art. **Turoe Stone** (*3m/5km N*) is a good example of La Tène art. The large round stone dates from the first century BC and is covered in ornamental carving. The area around the lough from which the town gets its name has yielded many *crannógs* (lake dwellings).

GALWAY (129m/206km)

The ancient City of the Tribes and principal city of Connacht has a beautiful location on the Atlantic coast at the foot of Lough Corrib. Approaching the station there are many delightful views of the much celebrated Galway Bay. The city is convenient to Connemara, the Gaeltacht (Irish speaking regions) and the Aran Islands.

There has been a town on this spot from at least the 12th century. It grew into a prosperous trading centre and developed strong links with Spain and the continent. Today Galway is a bustling university city with a reputation for high living.

Eyre Square is the centre of Galway, its park being named after John F. Kennedy, who addressed the people of Galway from it during his Irish visit. No. 19 Eyre Square (now a bank) displays the silver sword and great mace of the city (open bank hours). **St Nicholas' Church** (off Shop Street) dates from 1320 and is remarkably intact with a display of medieval artifacts. Columbus is said to have prayed in the church before setting out for America. In summer there is a *Son et Lumière* show here telling the story of Galway (details, TIO). **Spanish Arch** dates from 1594 and is named after the many Spanish merchants resident in the city in the past whose ships unloaded at the nearby quay. Spanish Parade and Long Walk make a beautiful evening stroll. **City Museum** (beside Spanish Arch) has a good collection of antiquities relating to Galway's varied history. There is a lovely view of the city and the bay from the roof (Jun-Sept, Mon-Sat, 10.00-17.00; Sun, 14.30-17.00).

Lynch's Castle, Shop Street, is the best preserved example of a 16th-century merchant's house (open bank hours). Note the ornamented windows and family crest outside. The **Lynch Memorial**, Market Street, consists of a skull and crossbones marking the site of the old jail. The inscription reads: 'To the stern and unbending justice of the chief magistrate of this city, James Lynch Fitzstephen, elected mayor AD 1493 who condemned and executed his own guilty son, Walter, on this spot'. The Lynches were one of the 14 tribes who played such a prominent role in the commercial and political life of the city from the 1200s. The others were: Athys, Blakes, Bodkins, Brownes,

D'Arcys, Deans, fforts, ffrenches, Kirwans, Joyces, Martins, Morrisses and Skerretts.

Claddagh The fishing village which created the famous Claddagh betrothal ring of two hands clasping a heart is now greatly changed. The thatched cottages are gone and there is little of historic interest to be seen. The copper-domed **Cathedral**, University Road, was completed in 1965. Its abundance of marble and granite has delighted some and horrified others; judge for yourself. **University College**, founded in 1849, has many rare items including the minutes of Galway Corporation going back 300 years. The College has a thriving Irish faculty and is known for its work in marine biology.

Walks: Galway is an easy and delightful city to explore on foot. Its winding streets have numerous alleyways and lanes which make a fascinating ramble. Try O'Gorman's Lane (behind St Nicholas'), Kirwan's Lane, (off Cross Street) or Buttermilk Lane (off Shop Street). You'll find many unusual shops and the sound of merriment and song from the multitude of pubs.

Theatre: The Druid Theatre, Chapel Lane, has a deservedly excellent reputation for presenting the work of Irish playwrights. Tel. (091) 68617. **Taiobhdhearc na Gaillimhe**, Middle Street, puts on Irish language productions all year round and in the summer a show of traditional music and dance. Tel. (091) 62024.

Around Galway:

Aran Islands The three islands, Inishmore, Inishmaan and Inisheer, 30m/48km out in the Atlantic, are renowned for their unchanged lifestyle and rugged scenery. The landscape is harsh and unyielding and Irish is the everyday language. Much in evidence is the traditional clothing of elaborately patterned Aran pullover and hat, *bainín* white woollen coat, the *críos* — a brightly coloured belt — and *pampooties*, leather shoes without a heel.

Among the sights is the amazing **Dun Aengus**, a large semi-circular prehistoric fort perched on the cliff edge of Inishmore 300 ft/90 m above the Atlantic. It is believed that the fort was originally twice the present size but that half fell into the sea. The landscape of the islands is marked by a web of distinctive dry stone walls which separate the small holdings and there are many Christian and pre-Christian remains to be found on all three islands.

The writer John Millington Synge spent some time between 1898 and 1902 on Inishmaan, making it the setting for his play *Riders to the Sea*. The museum there has many of his personal effects (open daily, 11.30-16.00 in summer). On Inisheer are the two cottages built by Robert Flaherty for his classic film *Man of Aran*.

Getting to the Aran Islands: regular CIE ferry from Galway docks all year round, tel. CIE Galway or TIO. Shorter summer only sailings from Rossaveal (26m/42km W; bus from Galway) and Doolin, Co. Clare. Details from TIO. Aer Arann operates frequent daily flights from Galway to all three islands, tel. (091) 65119.

Salthill *3m/5km SE; bus from Eyre Square.* This is a popular seaside resort on the shores of Galway Bay with lots of sports and bathing facilities.

Spiddal/An Spideal *7m/11km W; bus from Galway station.* There are lovely views across the bay to the Clare coast from this very pleasant beach resort in the middle of the Gaeltacht.

Carraroe *28m/45km W; bus from Galway.* The Carraroe bus runs through the rugged countryside of south Galway to terminate near the Coral Strand, one of the many excel-

Maamturk Mountains, Connemara

lent beaches in the area. Further west are the famine relief work bridges to the islands of Lettermore and Gorumna (infrequent bus to islands).

Carna *50m/80km W approx; bus from Galway.* The bus to Carna and Moyrus wanders through the splendid Connemara countryside with many craggy islands and sandy inlets to be seen on the way. There is good fishing and bathing to be had all round Kilkieran Bay.

Clifden via Maam Cross *49m/78.5km W; bus from Galway.* The main road from Galway to Clifden takes in some of the West's most spectacular scenery. The route was once served by a celebrated railway from Galway, traces of which can be seen on the way.

Heading north-west the road passes numerous small lakes on the right and flat bogland on the left. This was the stronghold of the O'Flahertys, whose castle at Aughnanure *(3m/5km E of Oughterard)* stands guard at a strategic point near the Corrib (open daily, 10.00-19.00 in summer). **Oughterard** *17m/27km.* A very pleasant riverside town noted for angling, boating and craft shops; known as the gateway to Connemara. The road from here to **Maam Cross** *(10m/16km)* passes through varied and superbly beautiful scenery; note in particular the mountain peaks on the right. **Recess** *27m/43km.* Delightful setting beneath the Twelve Bens, a distinctive group of mountains to the north. Soon after Recess the road passes Derryclare Lough, on whose shores much of the famous Connemara marble is found.

Clifden *49m/78.5km.* Sitting prominently between the mountains and the Atlantic, Clifden is known as the 'capital of Connemara'. It is noted for good seafood and traditional crafts and tweeds.

Cleggan *8m/13km NW; bus from Clifden.* There are several good beaches near the little harbour which is the embarkation point for Inishbofin Island.

Sky Road Absolutely magnificent coastal walk from Clifden to Scardaun *(8m/12km)* with unsurpassed views of the mountains and numerous offshore islands.

Connemara National Park, Letterfrack *9m/14.5km NE; bus from Clifden.* This vast park is well worth exploring for its gentle walks, nature trails and superb views. A Visitors' Centre has multi-media information on the whole Connemara region. About 6m/9.5km NW is **Renvyle House**, the former home of Oliver St John Gogarty, now a hotel. There are many letters and other personal effects associated with the writer and his many distinguished guests. The nearby **Renvyle Castle** looks out to sea and was once a fortress of the Joyces, O'Flahertys and Blakes.

Killary Harbour *bus from Galway to Leenane.* The superbly beautiful Killary Harbour resembles a huge fjord with a lakeside road running at the foot of the mountains for 3m/5km to the top of the harbour. Close by the Ashleagh Falls tumble down into the bay near the pretty village of Delphi. The road along the north side of Killary is equally spectacular.

Cong *25m/40km N; bus from Galway.* Set between Lough Mask and Lough Corrib, the village where the jewel-encrusted Cross of Cong was found is a peaceful spot. The Cross was made in 1123 in Roscommon for Turlough O'Conor and is now in the National Museum, Dublin.

An underground channel connects Lough Mask and Lough Corrib. It can be reached at several points, such as the Pigeon Hole, 1m/1.5km N of the town. Nearby is the curious Dry Canal, excavated as famine relief work in the last century. On completion it drained immediately through the highly porous bedrock as if someone had pulled the plug.

Clarenbridge *8m/13km SE; bus from Galway.* Clarenbridge is a place to enjoy superb oysters from the unspoilt
waters of Galway Bay and is the location of the annual
Galway Oyster Festival (Sept).

Dunguaire Castle *16m/26km S; bus from Galway to Kin-*
varra. This well restored 16th-century castle on a rock
overlooking Galway Bay now hosts nightly banquets with
Irish music, dancing and recitations. (Castle open daily,
April-Sept, 10.00-17.00; details of banquets and special
coaches from TIO Galway).

Dublin-Westport/Ballina

3 trains per day; fastest journey 3 hours 30 minutes;
166m/266km.

Trains to Westport now operate from Heuston Station,
Dublin. At Athlone the train leaves the Galway line, heading north-west via Roscommon and Claremorris to terminate on the shores of Clew Bay. The Ballina branch is
served from Claremorris with the occasional through train
from Dublin.

HEUSTON STATION (Kingsbridge) *buses 24, 79 from*
city centre; bus 90 from Connolly Station.
For Heuston-Portarlington see Dublin-Cork line. For Port-
arlington-Athlone see Dublin-Galway line.
After crossing the Shannon bridge at Athlone and passing
through the disused Midland Great Western Station the
train swings to the right and heads north-west through
rather flat bogland for some distance.

ROSCOMMON (101m/162km)
Overlooking the town on a hill are the massive ruins of
Rosscommon Abbey, built in 1268 by Sir Robert de
Ufford, the Lord Justice of Ireland. It was fought over
and sacked on a number of occasions. The jail survives
intact today and once boasted a hangwoman (or hangper-
son) as executioner in residence. It is presently occupied
by the tourist board.

CASTLEREA (117m/187km)
Very pleasantly sited on the banks of the River Suck,
Castlerea (pronounced Castleree) was the birthplace of Sir
William Wilde, a medical man of high repute and father
of the celebrated Oscar Wilde. **Clonalis House**, just outside the town, is the home of the O'Conor Don, descended
directly from the last high king of Ireland who reigned
until 1169. The superb 19th-century mansion is well worth
a visit for its fine library of books and Gaelic manuscripts,
as well as china and glassware. Aamong its treasures is the
harp owned by Turlough O'Carolan the blind harpist (b.

1670) whose delightful music is well known and available
on record and tape.

BALLYHAUNIS (129m/206km)

CLAREMORRIS (140m/224km)
Change here for Ballina.

CASTLEBAR (155m/248km)
The county town of Mayo is a busy commercial centre
with an attractive Mall or town square surrounded by
trees. Pleasure flights can be taken from Castlebar Airport,
tel. (091) 22853. Each October the Castlebar International
Song Contest attracts entries from all over the world;
details from TIO.

Ballintubber Abbey *9m/14.5km S; bus from Castlebar.*
Lovely church founded 1500 years ago. The present building was erected in the 13th century and has been carefully
and thoroughly restored as a parish church. The main
doorway, cloister, choir and windows are particularly
worth seeing.

WESTPORT (166m/266km)
A very attractive town at the head of Clew Bay centred
on the tree-lined Mall with its short hump-backed bridges.
A good panorama of the whole town can be had from the
top of Tober Hill Street. The Quay was once the heart of
the thriving port and now has some interesting pubs and
good quality restaurants.

There are several hundred islands in Clew Bay, most
uninhabited, and cruises depart daily from the Quay (summer only; details from TIO).

Westport House *1.5m/2.5km W*. The seat of the Marquess
of Sligo is a very fine Georgian house built in the 1730s
by Richard Cassel. The entrance hall with its marble staircase is imposing and in the well-appointed rooms there is
an excellent collection of paintings, furniture and
antiques. There is a restaurant in the house and a zoo in
the grounds. Open daily, Apr-Oct.

Croagh Patrick *5m/8km W; bus to Murrisk.* The 2,500 ft/
760 m mountain stands out all over Clew Bay. It was here
that St Patrick spent the forty days of Lent in 441 and
banished snakes and serpents from Ireland (zoologists
report that the common grass snake survived the inter-
dict). An enormous pilgrimage to the summit takes place
on the last Sunday in July when thousands make the ascent
which is best approached from Murrisk Abbey. The view
from the top is breathtaking.

Clare Island *4m/6.5km offshore in Clew Bay; boats from
Westport.* This was the home and has the grave of Grace
O'Malley, Grainne Uaile, the 16th-century pirate queen
of Connacht. This able lady ruled a good part of what is
now Mayo and her feats are recorded in story and song.

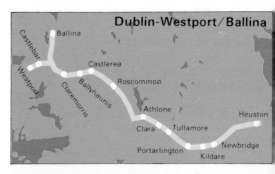

Dublin-Westport/Ballina

Ballina
Castlebar
Westport
Claremorris
Ballyhaunis
Castlerea
Roscommon
Athlone
Clara
Tullamore
Portarlington
Kildare
Newbridge
Heuston

On one occasion she met Elizabeth I in London, treating her as an equal.

Mulrany *18m/29km NW; bus from Westport.* The bus to Mulrany and Achill (*see below*) follows the coastline of Clew Bay and the route of a splendid railway which closed after a short life in 1937. Situated on an isthmus, Mulrany has an exceptionally mild climate and produces mediterranean-type flora.

Achill *27m/43km NW; bus from Westport takes different routes around the island.* The largest island in Ireland is in fact joined to the mainland by a bridge at Achill Sound. This is the main commercial centre of the island from where excursions by boat can be arranged. Achill is famous for its magnificent scenery, numerous tiny villages and unspoilt golden beaches. **Dugort**, lying beneath Slievemore Mountain, is a popular resort whose Seal Caves are accessible only by boat. The caves run far in under the mountain; boats for hire at the quay. **Keel** has excellent bathing on the large strand which stretches to the base of Minaun Cliffs. The sheer drop of 800 ft/240m to the sea is very popular with hang gliders. **Slievemore Village** near Keel is a real deserted village whose inhabitants were decimated or driven out by the famine. **Dooagh** is a fine sheltered village, little changed over the years. Keem Strand is a beautiful beach below Croghaun Mountain from which there are superb views. There is a straight drop at this point of 2,000ft/600m to the sea; it is advisable to stay away from the edge.

Unless travelling on one of the occasional through trains from Dublin, passengers for Ballina should change at Claremorris.

BALLINA (172m/275km)

This is a favourite anglers' town on the River Moy noted for salmon and trout fishing, just beyond the station is the **Dolmen of the Four Maols** which marks the 6th-century grave of four foster brothers who killed their master, Bishop Ceallach. They were executed and buried together under the dolmen.

Keem Bay, Achill Island

Killala *7m/11km NW; bus from Ballina.* The very pleasant Church of Ireland cathedral dates from 1670 and is flanked by an 80ft/25m round tower. Killala was the landing place of a French army under General Humbert in 1798 which came to grief at Ballinamuck, Co. Longford.

Belderg The bus from Ballina to Belderg (1 hr 30 mins) passes some of the most spectacular cliff scenery in Ireland between Ballycastle and Belderg; probably best explored on foot or by boat.

Belmullet *39m/63km W; bus from Ballina.* Small village at the head of the Mullet Peninsula. To really escape from it all stay on the bus (one per day in each direction) to Blacksod Point (2hrs 15mins) at the south end of the peninsula.

Dublin-Sligo

3 trains per day; fastest journey 3 hours 10 minutes; 136/218km; suburban service to Maynooth: 9 trains per day; journey time 30 minutes

The line to Sligo runs across the midlands to one of the most attractive and least explored parts of the country. Situated just south of Donegal and north-east of Connemara, Co. Sligo is often overlooked as a tourist destination by these two better-known regions but it will fully repay a visit in terms of beauty spots, sports facilities and holiday amenities. If you are interested in Irish writing then the county's close association with William Butler Yeats, Ireland's best-known poet, will make Sligo a must.

Note the distinctive grey limestone stations of the line's builders, the Midland Great Western Railway.

CONNOLLY STATION (Amiens Street)
After leaving the station the line immediately crosses the Royal Canal which opened 200 years ago to the Shannon with a branch to Longford. Although mainly disused, parts are being restored and it is hoped to reopen the entire waterway as a public amenity like the Grand Canal. The railway runs alongside the canal as far as Mullingar.

ASHTOWN (5m/8km)
The Phoenix Park *¼m/600 metres S; 10 bus from O'Connell Street* with 1,760 acres of open parkland is the largest city park in Europe. Nature trails, free roaming herds of deer, the President's house and the American Ambassador's, a fashionable race course, picnic spots, walks, views of the Liffey valley and the world famous Dublin Zoo are among the features of this enormous park.

CLONSILLA (9m/14km)
Outer suburban station, neatly restored after 20 years' closure.

LEIXLIP (13m/21km)
Lovely stretch of the River Liffey beside this neat village. Leixlip Castle (private) overlooks the salmon leap from which the town gets its name.

MAYNOOTH (17m/27km)
Castletown House, Celbridge *4m/6.5 km SE; 67 bus from Middle Abbey Street, Dublin,* is a superb Palladian mansion built in 1722 for Speaker Connolly of the Irish House of Commons. Marvellous plasterwork (Francini brothers), Venetian chandeliers and a good collection of prints, Irish furniture and paintings with all the trappings of a great house. Castletown should not be missed. Entrance at the eastern end of Main Street, through the gates and up a long tree-lined driveway. Apr-Sep, daily exc Tues, 11.00-18.00; Oct-Mar, Sun only, 14.00-17.00.

MULLINGAR (52m/83km)
The approach to this prosperous market town is through flat, boggy countryside and is dominated by the towers and cupola of the RC cathedral whose clock is the only

remnant of the original 1836 building. This is a good centre for angling in the many lakes nearby.

Lough Owel *3m/5km NW; bus from Mullingar.* A large lake visible on the left from the train with a number of attractive little islands covered in trees and offering bathing/boating facilities.

Tullynally Castle, Castlepollard, *13m/21km N; bus from Mullingar.* The ancestral home of the Pakenhams, the earls of Longford. The gardens are open June-Sept, 14.30-17.00 exc Sat; group tours of the castle by arr., tel. (044) 61159.

EDGEWORTHSTOWN (Mostrim) (70m/112km)
Named after the distinguished Edgeworth family which includes authors, scientists and inventors. The family home visible on the road into the town is now a nursing home. St John's church has a number of family momentoes of whom the most noted is probably Maria Edgeworth, author of *Castle Rackrent*.

LONGFORD (78m/125km)
Busy market and country town which has had a garrison for several hundred years.

Ballinamuck *14m/22.5km N; infrequent bus from Longford.* On a hill outside the village is a monument commemorating the final defeat of General Humbert and his Franco/Irish army by General Lake in 1798. The full story is told in Thomas Flanagan's *The Year of the French*; a melancholy spot.

DROMOD (89m/142km)
A quiet village with the cleanest pub in Ireland, the Breffni Inn, and a shop with an amazing collection of antiques, bric-a-brac and plain junk which flows out onto the roadside. Turn left at the T junction in the village and you can't miss it.

Fenagh *14m/22.5 km N; bus from Dromod.* The ruins of the abbey founded by St Columba have fine arched windows from which there are views of several surrounding counties.

Shortly after leaving Dromod the River Shannon comes into view on the left. The line crosses it at milepost 92 (147 km) and from here to Carrick there are delightful views of river and lakes on both sides of the line.

CARRICK-ON-SHANNON (100m/160km)
Leitrim's county town was established by James I in 1613. Set on low hills beside the Shannon with a lovely hump-backed road bridge, the town is now a major centre for cruisers which may be hired from the marina. There is also a boat rally each July.

Jamestown *3m/5km SE; bus from Carrick.* Once a walled town, as can be seen in the narrow town gate on the main

Carrick-on-Shannon, Co. Leitrim

street, and founded in 1625. It was named after James I.
Note the pretty little bridge on the Carrick side of the
town.

Drumshanbo *8m/13km N; bus from Carrick.* The An Tos-
tal festival takes place here each June, with music, ballads,
dancing, traditional songs, etc. The town is also a noted
angling centre, being positioned at the southern end of
Lough Allen which is surrounded by mountains. The
Dowra bus from Carrick runs along the eastern side of
the lake beside Slieve Anieran (Iron Mountain) and is a
good way to see the wild beauty of the area.

BOYLE *(107m/171km)*

Note the antique cartwheels and rural artifacts on display
in the well-maintained station. Boyle is a pleasant town
at the foot of the Curlew Mountains. The ruins of the
large 12th-century abbey are on the north side of the town
and are in a good state of preservation.

Lough Key Forest Park *2m/3km NE; bus from Boyle.* This
beautiful forest park consists of the former Rockingham
Estate and has walks, nature trails, camping, boating, a
restaurant, unusual shrubs and picnics spots. Moylurg
Tower, where the original Rockingham House stood,
gives splendid views of the countryside. Curiosities of the
estate include the haunted chapel, an ice house dug out
of a hill and an underground passage to enable servants
to approach the house without being seen. The island in
the lough contains the ruins of an old abbey and can be
reached easily by boat.

   The waterway from Carrick to Lough Key is one of the
loveliest in the country and the approach by cruiser is
spectacular.

Carrowkeel *8m/13km NW; bus from Boyle.* On the side of
the Bricklieve Mountains overlooking the numerous

islands of Lough Arrow is a group of cairns over 4,000 years old known as the Carrowkeel Passage Graves. On the far side of the lough, north of Kilmactranny, is the site of the battle of Moytura which took place fourteen centuries before Christ. During the engagement the Tuatha de Danaan defeated the Fir Bolgs. The area is strewn with large boulders and dolmens.

BALLYMOTE (122m/195km)
Note the extensive ruins and six towers of Ballymote Castle on the right as the train approaches the station. This was built in the 14th century for Richard de Burgh, the Red Earl of Ulster. In the **Franciscan Friary** in the town, now in ruins, the Book of Ballymote, a priceless illuminated manuscript, was compiled in 1391. It can now be seen in the Royal Irish Academy, Dublin.

COLLOONEY (130m/208km)
At one time this quiet town had three stations for connecting the West with Belfast and Scotland. It was the site of a skirmish between General Humbert and the Limerick militia in 1798.

SLIGO (136m/218km)
Sligo has a splendid position, surrounded by mountains, between Logh Gill and the Atlantic. From early times a place of strategic importance it is today a busy commercial centre with some of the most beautiful countryside very near at hand. The county is closely associated with W. B. Yeats who always had strong links with north-west Ireland.
Sligo Abbey (Abbey Street, key from no. 6) founded in 1252 and sacked in 1641 has very fine murals, statuary and windows. The cloisters which are almost intact contain beautiful arches and sculptured pillars. **Sligo Museum and Library** (Stephen Street, open Tues, Wed, Fri, Sat, 10.00-17.00; Thurs, 12.00-17.00) has a collection of paintings of the Yeats family, first editions of the poet's books as well as letters, diaries and handwritten poems.
Hawk's Well Theatre (Temple Street) is a highly regarded repertory theatre with a varied programme (tel. (071) 5336). **Yeats' Watch Tower** (corner of Adelaide/Wine Streets) is where the poet spent many childhood hours watching his grandfather's ships in the bay (to visit: contact Bon Furniture Co., Mon-Fri, 09.00-18.00).
Yeats International Summer School attracts visitors from all over the world each August for seminars, lectures, recitals; details from Yeats Memorial Building, Douglas Hyde Bridge, tel. (071) 2693.
Doorly Park Very pleasant walk along the Garravogue River from Douglas Hyde Bridge, Rockwood Parade, Kennedy Parade for fine views of Ben Bulben and Knocknarea.

Rosses Point *5m/8km NW; bus from Sligo station.* Popular seaside resort with championship golf course and excellent beaches on Sligo Bay.

Lough Gill *2m/3km E; bus from Sligo.* Exquisitely beautiful lake which rivals Killarney and is linked with Sligo by 2.5m/4km stretch of river lined on either side by delightful woods and parks. South of the river is a collection of ancient burial mounds (**Cairns Hill**) and the celebrated holy well of **Toberanalt** which attracts hundreds of pilgrims on the last Sunday of July. At the SE corner of Lough Gill is the island of **Innisfree**, the inspiration of Yeats' best-known poem. Near **Cottage Island** on the S shore is **Dooney Rock** immortalised in 'The Fiddler of Dooney' and there is a very pleasant nature trail close at hand. Cruises of the lake can be joined at the Riverside landing stage, tel. (071) 2540/2537.

Lissadell House *8m/13km NW; bus from Sligo.* This is the home of the Gore-Booth family, notably Eva, Countess Markievicz who was prominent in the 1916 Rising. The house dates from 1834 and has attractive drawing and music rooms. Yeats was a regular visitor. (Open May-Sept, weekdays, 14.30-17.15).

Drumcliffe *4m/6km N; bus from Sligo.* The simple grave of W. B. Yeats has a striking position nestling under Ben Bulben with the famous epitaph: 'Cast a cold eye on life, on death, horseman pass by.'

Strandhill *4m/6km W; bus from Sligo.* Sandy beaches galore facing Coney Island to which you can walk when the tide is out *(1m/1.5km).* A line of pillars marks the path. **Knocknarea** *(1m/1.5km S of Strandhill)* has a huge cairn on the hilltop, said to be the burial place of Maeve, the first century AD Queen of Connacht.

Carrowmore *2m/3km SW.* This hill has the largest collection of megalithic remains in Ireland or Britain consisting of dolmens, stone circles, cairns, burial chambers, etc.

Innishmurray Abandoned in 1947, this fascinating island has extensive monastic ruins (St Molaise's) dating back 1200 years as well as cashels, beehive huts, altars, holy wells, stations, cursing stones and a sweathouse. Bus from Sligo to Cliffoney *(14m/23km N)*, then 3m/5km to Mullaghmore for boat to Innismurray. Check at TIO beforehand.

Glencar *7m/11km NE; bus from Sligo.* Spectacular lakeland scenery featuring a waterfall with an unbroken fall of 50ft/15m.

Dublin-Dundalk-Belfast

Dublin-Dundalk: 11 trains per day; fastest journey 1 hour; 55m/88km

Dublin-Belfast: 6 trains per day; fastest journey 1 hour 55 minutes; 116m/186km

The line to Belfast is part of the former Great Northern Railway. Today it is operated jointly by CIE and Northern Ireland Railways. The route runs near the coast for a good part of the way via the industrial town of Drogheda, a centre for touring the many sights of the Boyne Valley (*see below*).

CONNOLLY STATION (Amiens Street)
See Howth-Bray line for Connolly Station-Howth Junction. No. 90 bus from Heuston Station.

PORTMARNOCK (7m/11km)
Magnificent 3m/5km beach in this expanding suburb (20 min walk from station). The championship golf course here is well known for the Carroll's Irish Open held each August.

MALAHIDE (9m/14km)
Very fine, well-maintained station building with elaborate ironwork evident on the platform. Near the station is the entrance to **Malahide Castle**, an impressive edifice which up to 1975 had been the home of the Talbot family for nearly 1,000 years. Now owned by Dubin County Council it has a superb collection of furniture and also the National Portrait collection, formerly in the National Gallery of Ireland. The Great Hall is the only perfect example of its type left in Ireland. Guided tours all year, 10.00-17.00, later in summer. The extensive parklands are open every day from 09.30-dusk.

Immediately after leaving the station the train appears to be running on water as it crosses a long viaduct over a sea inlet on which large numbers of birds can be seen.

DONABATE (12m/19km)

RUSH AND LUSK (14m/22km)
Market garden centre in rich farmland of north Co. Dublin. Rush is a small fishing village with fine beaches. Lusk has a well-preserved round tower which you can climb (key from nearby shop). The Good Old Days Museum, Channel Road, has numerous exhibits of past life in the country including old farming tools and machinery (summer, daily, 14.30-17.30; tel. (01) 437512/437638).
Lambay Island This privately-owned island, now a bird sanctuary, can be visited by boat from Rush. Lambay was the scene of the first Viking incursion in 795 and has the remains of unusual defence works still intact. Write in advance to: The Steward, Lambay Island, Rush, Co. Dublin.

SKERRIES (18m/29km)
An attractive seaside resort with bracing walks along the

Malahide Castle, Co. Dublin

seafront. Shenick's Island, just offshore, can be reached by foot at low tide. A pleasant walk along the cliffs brings you to the little fishing port and harbour of Loughshinny (3m/5km). 5m/8km out to sea the Rockabill Lighthouse is perched on a lonely rock.

From here the railway runs along the coast for 10m/16km as far as Laytown, with regular beaches and sea inlets.

BALBRIGGAN (22m/35km)
The approach to Balbriggan is very attractive as the train runs over a landscaped park and a river below. This resort is noted for its hot salt-water baths.

GORMANSTON (24m/38km)
The 1786 castle of Gormanston, now a school, is on the

site of a 14th-century mansion.

MOSNEY (26m/42km)
Summer-only station for the nearby holiday camp.

LAYTOWN (27m/43km)
A first-rate sandy beach runs from here to the mouth of the River Boyne at Mornington, making a superb 6m/9.5km walk (bus also from Laytown). It was on Laytown Strand that the Tara Brooch, a superb piece of gold jewellry from early Christian times, was found; it is now in the National Museum, Dublin.

Mornington (*bus from Laytown*) The Maiden Tower at the estuary is 400 years old, while nearby is the mini-obelisk known as the Lady's Finger.

DROGHEDA (32m/51km)
A very old town (2,000 years) on the river Boyne which

is today an industrial centre. The Normans erected a bridge here on the site of the ancient ford (*Droichead Atha* means the Town of the Ford) and a town developed on either side of the river. After a lengthy siege by Oliver Cromwell in 1649 most of the garrison, including Sir Arthur Aston, were massacred and the remainder transported to Barbados.

St Laurence's Gate is the only one of the original ten gates still standing and is in perfect condition. **St Peter's Church,** West Street, contains the embalmed head of Oliver Plunkett, the Archbishop of Armagh who was hanged at Tyburn, London in 1681.

Around Drogheda:
Inland from Drogheda the Boyne Valley and the surrounding area has a wealth of fascinating historic sites which are well worth exploring. All are accessible by one or more buses from Drogheda or in one or two cases directly by bus from Dublin.

Battle of the Boyne (site) *3.5m/5.5km W; bus from Drogheda*. In 1690 the Dutch king, William of Orange, defeated and deposed James II in battle, thus securing the English throne. The victory on the banks of the Boyne is celebrated with gusto by Northern Protestants each 12 July. The stump of an obelisk marks the spot where the Duke of Schomberg was killed leading a charge against the Stuart army.

Brugh na Boinne (palace of the Boyne) The ancient royal burial grounds of the Boyne valley, an area between Drogheda and Slane, have about 20 passage graves which are 4,500 years old. A visit to them is an unforgettable experience.

Dowth *5m/8km W; bus from Drogheda stops within 1m/1.5km*. This burial mound has a stone kerb all the way round with two passage graves which require some physical effort to enter.

Newgrange (2m/3km W from Dowth). Along a twisting, narrow road is the awe-inspiring tumulus of Newgrange, generally agreed to be the finest in Europe. The mound is 44 ft/13.5 m high, 260ft/80m across and its outer rim is embellished with massive stones. Twelve of the original pillar stones remain with a prominent ditch. At the base of the cairn there is a kerb of 97 stones. Distinctive spiral, concentric circles and other geometric patterns are much in evidence, in particular on the Threshold Stone. The main passage is 3ft/1m wide, 57ft/19m long and between 8-5ft/2.5-1.5m high and leads to the lofty central chamber with its three recesses.

Newgrange has been accurately dated as being built between 2,800 and 2,400 BC. One of its great mysteries, apart from the obvious architectural sophistication, is how it was possible to build the tumulus in such a way that on only one day of the year, the winter solstice (21 December), does daylight fall directly on the inner chamber floor. Newgrange is magical.

Guided tours start at the TIO beside the mound, where there is a small museum which tells the story of Newgrange. June-Sept, daily, 10.00-19.00; rest of year, 10.00-17.00; Sun, 14.00-17.00, tel. (041) 24274.

Knowth *2m/3km E of Slane; bus from Drogheda/Slane.* This mound has many unusual stone carvings but is at present closed while excavation of the site continues.

Slane *9m/14.5m W; bus from Drogheda.* Lovely little village with four identical houses diagonally opposite at the main cross-roads, said to have been built by a local landowner for his four precocious daughters. 1m/1.5km N is the **Hill of Slane** (500ft/150m) where in AD 433 St Patrick first proclaimed Christianity in Ireland by lighting the pascal fire in defiance of a pagan king. From the hill there are superb views of the whole of the Boyne Valley; also the remains of a 16th-century monastic school. **Slane Castle** (private), a regular venue for large-scale pop concerts, is just outside the town.

Trim *26m/42km SW; 28m/45km NW; bus from Dublin.* Marvellous old town on the Boyne with the largest Anglo-Norman castle in Ireland begun by Hugh de Lacy in 1173. The massive keep, 70ft/21m high, has four square towers with an outer wall of 500 yards/460m guarded by ten towers and a moat. The **Yellow Steeple** opposite the Castle is all that remains of the 13th-century Abbey of St Mary's. The **Town Hall**, Castle Street, holds the records of Trim from 1659.

Tara *6m/9.5km S of Navan; 24m/38.5km NW by bus from Dublin.* Tara of the Kings was for many years the capital of Ireland. Originally occupied by the kings of Meath it became the seat of the High Kings who held a *feis* (assembly) every three years to pass laws, settle disputes and maintain the peace. The last king to live at Tara was Malachy II who died in 1022.

The Lia Fáil (Stone of Destiny) is said to have been the coronation stone of the High King. Although only extensive mounds remain, Tara has lots of atmosphere and there are excellent views of Co. Meath from the top.

Kells *37m/59km W by bus from Drogheda via connection at Navan; 40m/64km NW by direct bus from Dublin.* St Columba founded a monastery here in the 6th century where the incomparable illuminated manuscript the *Book of Kells* was composed. This brilliantly illustrated book of the four gospels is now in the library of Trinity College, Dublin. In the town centre is the **High Cross**, (8 ft/2.5 m high)

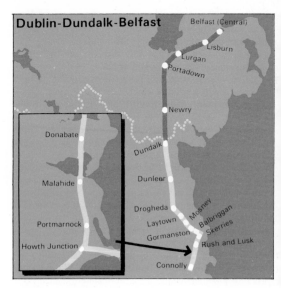

which has several detailed base panels. **St Columba's Church** (9th-century) is on the site of the original monastery and is similar to St Kevin's Church, Glendalough. The nearby round tower is 100 ft/30 m high and close to it are four more heavily ornamented High Crosses.

Mellifont *6m/9.5km NW; bus from Drogheda.* This was the first Cistercian Abbey in Ireland (1142) located on a beautiful river site. Only the substantial gatehouse, Chapter House and the unusual octagonal Lavabo where the monks washed before entering the refectory are still to be seen. There are also several richly carved columns and the lower part of a spiral staircase in the ruins of the church.

Monasterboice *6m/9.5km N; bus from Drogheda.* The chief item of interest in this 5th-century Benedictine monastic settlement is the superb **Muiredach's Cross** which is covered on all sides with the most elaborate carvings of scenes from the Old and New Testament. The Cross stands 16ft/5m and merits close inspection. Nearby are the ruins of two churches and a round tower which at one time was the tallest in Ireland.

Immediately after leaving Drogheda station the railway crosses the River Boyne by the magnificent Boyne Viaduct which towers high above ships loading at the quays far below. It is said that throwing a penny into the river when crossing the bridge brings luck. There are spectacular views to right and left from the Viaduct.

DUNLEER (42m/67km)

Skerries, Co. Dublin

DUNDALK (55m/88km)

Dundalk was once an important railway junction with trains running to Greenore, Clones, Enniskillen, Bundoran, Belfast and Dublin. Approaching the station on the left are the former workshops of the Great Northern Railway where many of its finest engines were built.

This is a busy commercial town and a good centre for touring the Cooley Peninsula, closely linked with the Ulster warrior Cuchulainn of the Red Branch Knights who was born and died near the town. A statue of this ferocious character can be seen in the GPO, Dublin.

Carlingford Lough is beautifully placed between the Cooley Mountains to the south and the Mourne Mountains to the north. A good way to see the beauties of the Lough is to take the bus from Dundalk-Carlingford-Omeath-Newry (1 hr 20 min).

Carlingford *15m/24km E; bus from Dundalk.* Delightful town spectacularly situated beside the lough. **King's John's Castle**, built in 1210 to protect the harbour, is now a substantial ruin. **Taaffe's Castle**, Newry Street, is a 16th-century tower in good repair with a fine spiral staircase to the battlements. **The Mint** where coins for local use were minted is a well preserved 15th-century building with elaborate carved windows. **The Tholsel** was once the town gate, later a jail, and now forms an arch over the road.

The border between the Republic and Northern Ireland *(59.5m/95km)* is indicated by two white posts on the left hand side. The railway continues from here to Portadown *(87m/139km)* and Belfast Central *(116m/186km)*.

Railways in Northern Ireland

The lines currently used by Northern Ireland Railways (NIR) formerly made up the separate services of the Great Northern Railway (GNR), the Northern Counties Railway (NCC) and the Belfast and County Down Railway (BCDR), three companies formed in the mid-nineteenth century by the amalgamation of smaller concerns. Belfast Central Station was built in the late 1970s, and replaced the old Queen's Quay and Great Victoria Street stations, while York Road Station, the former NCC terminus, was modernised and remains in use for Larne line trains. A frequent bus service operates between the two stations, stopping in Belfast city centre en route.

Abbreviations

Some suggestions for places to eat have been included in this section and abbreviations used as follows: **S** for snack meals, **P** for pub grub and **R** for restaurants. Additional abbreviations are BH (Bank Holiday), C (Roman Catholic), CI (Church of Ireland), EC (Early Closing) and NT (National Trust).

Telephone Numbers of principal Railway Stations and Enquiry Offices

Antrim 63185
Ballymena 2277
Ballymoney 63241
Bangor 454141
Belfast:
Train enquiries 230310
Travel centre 230671
Carrickfergus 63286
Coleraine 2263

Larne:
Harbour 73616
Town 72347
Travel centre 70517
Lisburn 2294
Londonderry 42228
Lurgan 22052
Newry 69271
Portadown 333051
Whitehead 72377

Belfast

Six day shopping. TIO: Northern Ireland Tourist Board, High Street, tel: 231221, all year. Belfast Airport, tel: Crumlin 52103, all year. Irish Tourist Board: 53 Castle Street, Belfast, tel: 227888. If travelling within the city boundary always use Citybus (red). Ulsterbus (blue) runs no internal city service. Bus enquires: Great Victoria Street bus station, tel: 220011. Taxis: Donegall Square East, Central Station, York Road Station. Youth Hostel: 11 Saintfield Road, tel: 647865.

Capital of Northern Ireland, attractively situated on the Lagan estuary at the foot of the Antrim plateau. Despite its relative decline as an industrial force, and more particularly the toll taken by the Troubles, Belfast is a vigorous city, much of which is extremely pleasing to the eye. It also has a fine cultural tradition which is not always recognised, and its museums and art galleries repay close inspection.

Major Festivals: Belfast Arts Festival: three week culture feast, with something for everyone. Local and international artists, enormous variety of music, theatre, film. *Nov, details: Belfast 665577 or Belfast TIO.* Circuit of Ireland international car rally: start and finish, *Apr.* Royal Ulster Agricultural Society, Kings Hall, Balmoral: annual agricultural show, *May.* July 12 Parades: marking the anniversary of the Battle of the Boyne in 1690. Ancient Order of Hibernians' parades, *Aug 15.*

CATHEDRALS & CHURCHES

St Anne's Cathedral (CI), *Donegall Street;* plain but impressive modern building. **St Malachy's Church** (C), *Alfred Street:* excellent fan-vaulted ceiling. **Unitarian church**, *Rosemary Street:* fine plasterwork, woodwork.

The city has many other fine religious buildings, mostly from the second half of the 19th c, when some seventy new churches were established. Perhaps the most notable are Fitzroy Presbyterian (1872), *University Street;* St Mary's (1869), *Crumlin Road;* St Thomas's (1870), *Lisburn Road;* Elmwood Hall, deconsecrated church, *by Botanic Gardens;* the small, delightful St Matthew's, *Woodvale Road,* which includes an imitation round tower; St Mark's, *Dundela,* completed in 1878 to design by William Butterfield.

NOTABLE BUILDINGS

City Hall, *Donegall Square:* handsome structure with a fine marble interior, wall murals, excellent city views from dome. *Guided tours, Fri, 10.30 a.m. Details: 220202.* **Stormont,** *E Belfast, 22, 23 Citybus to Massey Avenue, 16, 17, 20 to main entrance.* Commanding building in 300 acres of gardens, seat of NI parliament from 1921–72. Superb views from terrace, good walks. Stormont Castle, recently the NI Prime Minister's official residence, is nearby. **Belfast Castle,** *N Belfast, 2, 3, 4, 5, 6, 45 Citybus.* Attractive walks in extensive grounds; if you feel nimble, a shepherd's path winds up Cave Hill to McArt's Fort on the summit.

Custom House, *High Street:* majestically proportioned building set where the culverted Farset joins the Lagan. Anthony Trollope worked here as a surveyor's clerk in 1841. **Royal Courts of Justice,** *Chichester Street:* a substantial structure, in Portland Stone, opened in 1933 as a gift from Westminster.

Linenhall Library, *Donegall Square North:* late 18th c, now fully refurbished, very strong on Irish interest material, occasional exhibitions. *Tues-Fri, Sat a.m. Details: 224579.* **Queen's University,** *University Road:* founded 1849, attractive main building; library with over 750,000 books, various collections, including Hamilton Harty music. By arr., librarian.

MUSEUMS

Ulster Museum and Art Gallery, *Stranmillis Road, 65, 69, 71 Citybus.* Distinguished collection of art and antiquities, including treasure from the *Girona,* a Spanish Armada galleon wrecked off N Antrim coast. Coelacanth, rare preserved specimen of 'living fossil' fish. Permanent art collection featuring many fine modern works and such Irish artists as William Conor, Jack B. Yeats, Colin Middleton, George Campbell. Sculpture by Henry Moore, Barbara Hepworth, F. E. McWilliam. Visiting exhibitions. Engineering hall has working examples of old machinery. Monthly poster lists all museum activities. *Café. Mon-Fri, 10 a.m.–5 p.m. Sat, 1 p.m.–5 p.m. Sun, 2 p.m.–5 p.m. Details: 668251.*

GALLERIES

Caldwell Gallery, *Bradbury Place, 41, 52, 59, 65, 69, 71, 83, 85, 89 Citybus; train to Botanic Station.* Large, attractive basement gallery with regular exhibitions by

Irish and British artists, *Mon–Fri, 10 a.m.–5 p.m. Tel: 223226.* **Arts Council Gallery**, *Bedford House, Bedford Street:* frequent exhibitions by local and international artists, *Mon–Sat, 10 a.m.–5 p.m. Details: 663591.* **Octagon Gallery**, *Lower Crescent, 83, 85 Citybus; train to Botanic Station.* Regular exhibitions of paintings, sculpture, craft work from local sources. *Tues–Sat, 11 a.m.–5 p.m. Tel: 246259.* **Malone Gallery**, *32 Malone Road, 71 Citybus.* Regular exhibitions with special emphasis on young, local artists, *Mon–Fri, 10 a.m–5 p.m. Tel: 662169.* **Bell Gallery**, 13 Adelaide Park, 71 Citybus. Irish artists' work, rare editions of Irish books, crafts, antique furniture, *Mon–Fri, 10 a.m.–5 p.m. Sat, 10 a.m.–1 p.m. Tel: 662998.* **Gallery 667**, *667 Lisburn Road:* occasional exhibitions.

THEATRES

Grand Opera House, *Gt Victoria Street:* designed by 19th c theatre architect Frank Matcham, reopened in 1980 after a thorough refurbishing. Gloriously rococo interior complete with old-style stage safety curtain. Drama, opera, ballet, pantomime. *Details: 241919.* **Lyric Players' Theatre**, *Ridgeway Street, Stranmillis, 69 Citybus.* Fine, modern theatre offers modern and classical drama, with a generally Irish emphasis. Food bar, occasional lectures, recitals. *Details: 60081.* **Arts Theatre**, *Botanic Avenue, 83, 85 Citybus; train to Botanic Station.* Wide range of drama, seasonal childrens' shows, rock musicals, emphasis on entertainment. *Details: 224936.* **Group Theatre**, *Bedford Street;* amateur drama. *Details: 229685.*

ROUND & ABOUT

Belfast Zoo, *Antrim Road:* superb collection of animals and birds, a magnet for children. Guided tours, film shows, lectures. *Mar–Oct, 10 a.m.–6 p.m. daily. Nov–Feb, 10 a.m.–4 p.m. daily. Last admission 1 hr before closing. Café. Details: 776277.*

   Falls Road/Shankill Road, *Belfast, 13, 14, 15, 39, 55, 63 Citybus.* World famous, not to say notorious, the militantly Unionist Shankill, and Nationalist Falls are areas of considerable personality, and not without appeal. In the City centre the narrow passageways between Anne Street and High Street still have a little of their original 18th c atmosphere and at **Harland and Wolff** *(16, 20, 21, 22, 24, 26 Citybus),* where the 'Titanic' was built, you will find 'Goliath' and 'Samson'

Palm House, Botanic Gardens, Belfast

the world's 2nd and 3rd biggest cranes. *By arr. PR Dept.* University area: pleasant walks, including University Square, Upper and Lower Crescent. Gilnahirk Road, *E Belfast, 76, 77 Citybus to Gilnahirk Road:* good 20 minute climb up into Castlereagh Hills, with superb views over N Co. Down, as far as Isle of Man in clear weather. Belmont Road, *E Belfast, 22, 23 Citybus to Belmont Road:* invigorating walks in Holywood Hills. **Albert Clock:** *High Street,* built 1851.

Variety Market, *next to Law Courts, Chichester Street.* All kinds of everything. *Every Fri.* Smithfield Market, *behind Royal Avenue:* the present prefabricated shops lack the character of the old market, burned down some years ago, but the bargains are as good.

The Crown Liquor Saloon (NT), *Great Victoria Street:* high Victorian style pub, snugs, gloriously over-the-top glass and tilework and a thoroughly distinctive atmosphere. **Robinsons**, *next door:* snugs, tile work, good Guinness and interesting old prints. **Kelly's Cellars**, *Bank Place, off Royal Avenue:* one of Belfast's oldest pubs, dating back some 200 years, with character to match.

Kings Hall, *Balmoral, 59 Citybus or train.* Exhibition Centre, *details TIO.* **Ulster Hall**, *Bedford Street:* regular Ulster Orchestra, rock and pop concerts. *Orchestral bookings: Arts Council Gallery, Bedford Street, tel: 663591.*

PARKS

Botanic Gardens, *near Ulster Museum, 69, 71, 83, 85 Citybus.* Acres of pleasant space, highlight is the Victorian Palm House, an elegant structure in curved glass. *Daily from 7.30 a.m. to lighting-up time.* Dixon Park, *Upper Malone, S Belfast, 71 Citybus.* Setting for internationally renowned rose trials every summer. Ormeau Park, *78, 82, 83, 85 Citybus.* Fine expanse between Ormeau and Ravenhill Roads, Old Waterworks, *Antrim Road, 2, 3, 4, 5, 6, 45 Citybus.* Now an attractive park with waterfalls and bridges. Minnowburn Beeches, *on S fringe of Belfast, in Lagan valley:* good walks in fields, woodland, open spaces, *best approached on B205 to Shaw's Bridge.* Lagan Regional Park, starts at Molly Ward's lock on Stranmillis embankment, near Botanic gardens, and continues for 8 m (13 km) to Lisburn; including Barnett's demesne, *71 Citybus:* delightfully wooded part overlooking River Lagan. Hazelwood Park, *next to zoo:* delightful setting with lake. Summer entertainment.

Belfast – Londonderry

BELFAST CENTRAL

BOTANIC

LISBURN

KNOCKMORE

BALLINDERRY

GLENAVY
Pretty one-street village sloping down to Glenavy River.

Giant's Causeway, Co. Antrim

Around Glenavy:

Ram's Island: off Sandy Bay, W of B12 near Glenavy. Interesting Lough Neagh island, complete with stump of round tower. Wooded bird sanctuary. Ideal for a peaceful picnic.

Boat hire, Tunny Cut, between Glenavy and Aghalee.

CRUMLIN

Quiet, pleasant village at head of wooded Crumlin Glen. Good walks alongside tiny Crumlin River, which forms cascades after the weir. The Glen has a 'Cockle House', a 19th-century folly built partly as a house, partly as a cave. Largest opening faces Mecca! 13th-century church ruins by Pound bridge over river.

Quail and Ornamental Pheasant Garden, 2 Crumlin Rd. All year, daily, 2–6 p.m. Closed Thurs; Sun by arr., tel. 52900.

ANTRIM

A pleasant if unremarkable town at the NE corner of Lough Neagh, founded on the site of an ancient monastery. Although Antrim is largely residential, it has points of interest and excellent sporting facilities. EC Wed.

Round Tower: about 1,000 years old, remarkably well preserved.

Antrim Castle Demesne: fine gardens W of town along Lough Neagh shore, laid out in late 17th century in similar style to Versailles, complete with ornamental waters. Only a tower remains of original castle, burned in 1922, during previous Troubles. Beside it, the Norman motte makes a fine viewpoint. Co. Antrim agricultural show held here in July.

Clotworthy House, castle grounds: theatre, exhibitions, details from Belfast TI0.

Alexander Irvine's Cottage, Pogue's Entry, off Church St: 18th century cottage, childhood home of the author of the 19th-century classic, *My Lady of the Chimney Corner*. Interior little changed, key from adjoining shop.

Lough Neagh cruises: Antrim Marina, Sixmilewater, May-Sept, daily, details tel. 64131.

S *Castle,* 51 High St.

P *Bailiwick Inn,* Market Square.

R *Clonavon House,* 64 Fountain St, tel. 63405.

Around Antrim:

Dunadry Inn, hotel and restaurant: 3m (5km) SE of

Antrim; 120 bus from Antrim. Created from an 18th-century linen mill and its cottages. Axles from the mill's beetling machinery were used to form the gallery's pillars.

Randalstown Forest: deer, squirrels and water birds to be seen from hides. Visiting permits from the Forestry Division, Dundonald House, Belfast BT4 3SB, or forester at Tardree.

Shane's Castle Demesne: 2m (3km) W of Antrim on A6T. Nature reserve with steam railway running 1½m (2½km) round demesne. Two hides by shore of Lough Neagh; café and picnic sites. Excellent facilities for a full day out. Easter; Apr-May, Sun, BH; June, Wed, Sat, Sun; July-Aug, Tues, Wed, Thurs, Sat, Sun, BH; Sep, Sun; 12-6p.m. Car rally, June. Steam rally, July. Details, tel: 63380.

Toomebridge: 10m (16km) W of Antrim; 210, 211 bus from Antrim. Eel fishery, run as a co-op. Spring is best time to visit, when about 20 million elvers (baby eels) swim across Atlantic and up the River Bann.

P *Elk Bar*, 40 Hillhead Rd.

R *Solitude*, 174 Moneynick Rd, tel. Magherafelt 50230.

BALLYMENA

Prosperous town with a strong Scottish influence, which may account for it having been described—not entirely fairly—as the meanest town in Ireland. Excellent game fishing. EC Wed (all day). Bus enquiries: bus station, Galgorm Rd, tel. 2214.

St Patrick's (CI), Castle St, is noted for its rich, interior and 19th-century Art Nouveau windows. From Ballymena, roads run through the Braid and Clogh valleys to Antrim moorlands. The coastal routes to Cushendun and Cushendall are very attractive.

S *Cameron's Coffee Shop*, 23 Broughshane St.

P *Raglan*. 20 Queen St.

R *Adair Arms* (also hotel), Ballymoney Rd. tel. 3674.

Around Ballymena:

Broughshane: 3m (5km) NE of Ballymena; 128 bus from Ballymena. Memorial in Rathcavan church yard to the locally-born ancestors of General Sam Houston, who brought Texas into the US. There is a pleasant walk near the village, across the Buttermilk Footbridge by River Braid.

Gracehill: 2m (3km) W of Ballymena; 127 bus from Ballymena; Founded by Moravians in 18th century. German Christmas customs still observed in the village church. Ask rector to see Moravian church records.

Kells: midway between Antrim and Ballymena; 149 bus from Ballymena. Pleasant walk round Diamond and across the old bridge with views over the weir on the Kells Water River. Remains of ancient Augustinian abbey.

Portglenone: 215 bus from Ballymena. The Cistercian Monastery has its own printing press. Male visitors only. Details, tel. 821211.

Portglenone Forest: 8m (13km) W of Ballymena. Bannside oak woods, with Augustine Henry trail, in honour of the forestry pioneer born nearby in 1857, and a memorial grove with some of the thousands of trees and shrubs he discovered. Two holy wells. Picnic sites, nature trails.

CULLYBACKEY

Arthur Cottage, Dreen, home of the parents of Chester Alan Arthur, 21st President of the USA in early 1880s. Fully restored, with typical 19th-century furnishings, picture gallery. Good view of the River Main. Apr–Sept 30, daily, 2–6 p.m. Closed Fri.

1m (2km) N of village on Glarryford road is a curious beehive-shaped thatched cottage.

BALLYMONEY:

All day closing Mon. TIO, Lower Main St, tel. Bushmills 31343. Two interesting churches: Our Lady and St Patrick (C), built of local basalt, fine stained-glass windows. Trinity Presbyterian Church, built 1884 by Home Rule advocate Rev. J. B. Armour.

S *Chat & Chew*, 9 Victoria St.

P *Bush Tavern*, 15 Market St.

R *Bubbles*, 9 Main St, tel. 62956.

COLERAINE

Passengers change here for Portrush (via Cromore and Dhu Varren – some trains run through, so check at station before setting off).

Said to have been given its name by St Patrick in the 5th century, Coleraine became a small city during the Middle Ages, and though there are few remains from this period, there are a number from its second incarnation, as a plantation town, including remnants of the 1641 seige, also fine Georgian houses and streets.

More recently it became a university town, with the controversial siting of the University of Ulster.

St Patrick's Church (CI), town centre: see mark on N wall where cannon ball hit building during 1641.

Town Hall: relics include sword presented by Irish Society in 1616. Mon–Fri, by arr.

Tropical Bird Garden, Ballymoney Rd: daily.

Walks: good along both banks of River Bann.

Anderson Park, by river: a quiet if windy oasis by the main shopping area.

University of Ulster: many arts events throughout the year. Concerts in Diamond Hall, smaller recitals and visual arts exhibitions in the Octogon. Guided tours mid-July–mid-Aug, Wed, 11 a.m. Details and bookings, Cashier's Office, tel. 4141 extn. 278. Library of some 200,000 volumes inc. Denis Johnston manuscripts and much material relating to World Wars I and II. Term time, Mon–Fri, 9 a.m.–10 p.m., Sat, 9 a.m.–1 p.m. Vacations, Mon–Fri, 9 a.m.–5 p.m.

Riverside Theatre, amateur and professional productions, touring art exhibitions in foyer. Details and bookings, tel. 51388.

Guy Wilson Daffodil Garden, with almost 1,500

Downhill Strand and Mussenden Temple

varieties of daffodil, the world's most comprehensive collection.

S *Coffee Cup* , Queen St.

P *Tommy's Bar*, 10 Market St.

R *Old Forge Inn*, 6 New Market St, tel. 52931.
Salmon Leap, 53 Castleroe Rd, tel. 2992.

Around Coleraine:

The Cutts: 2m (3km) S of Coleraine. Salmon leap. Nearby, Somerset forest recreation area. Also huge Mountsandel mound on E bank of Bann, site of a 1st-century royal palace.

Dervock: 5m (7km) NE of Ballymoney; 171 bus from Coleraine. EC Sat. Farm outhouse at Conagher was home of great-great grandfather of US president William McKinley, assassinated in 1901.

R *North Irish Horse*, 15 Main St, tel. 41205.

Dundarave: just N of Bushmills. Splendid Georgian house with sumptuous interior. By arr. only, tel. Ballycastle 62225/22565.

CASTLEROCK

Bracing seaside village just N of Bann estuary. Good beach , and open air swimming pool. TIO, Main St, tel. 258. EC Wed or Sat.

R *Golf*, 17 Main St, tel. 848204.

Around Castlerock:

Bann Estuary Wildlife Sanctuary: 3m (5km) E of Castlerock. Observation hide with illustrative panels. The River Bann is navigable by boats wiih draughts of up to 3ft (1 metre) all the way from sea to Portadown, crossing Lough Neagh. Unusual, little-used way of seeing a cross-section of Ulster life.

Downhill Castle: near Mussenden Temple. Built about 1780 and once the setting of magnificent social gatherings and a great art collection. Impressive even in its dilapidation.

Downhill Forest: W of Downhill demesne. Good walks in department of Agriculture property. Nearby Portadvantage Cove is haven of peace.

Mussenden Temple, entrance by Bishop's Gate. Built 1783, spectacularly sited above Magilligan Strand. Excellent walks in nearby glen, particularly in early summer when the daffodils and rhododendrons are in full bloom. Apr–Sept, daily, except Fri.

BELLARENA

Home of the Ulster Gliding Club. 'Miners' Marks', two small towers mark where first Ordnance Survey of Ireland and Britain was begun in 1934.

Around Bellarena:

Magilligan Strand: Ireland's longest strand runs for 6m (10km), starting just W of Castlerock. Also Martello tower, built during Napoleonic Wars.

LONDONDERRY

Perhaps more popularly known as Derry (the city's rightful title is a matter of political debate). Settlement began in the 6th century, and certain historical events, such as the lifting of the siege in 1689, are still recalled with passion. A walk from Guildhall Square, through the William St area as far as Free Derry Corner, with its internationally-known legend, 'You are now entering Free Derry', will give a vivid illustration of this intensely Irish city's turmoil. With the old W part of the city rising dour and cramped from the edge of the River Foyle, Derry may appear at first sight unwelcoming; closer acquaintance will reveal the very opposite. TIO, Foyle St, tel. 269501. EC Thurs. Bus enquiries, Foyle St bus station, tel. 262261.

Guildhall, Shipquay Place: built 1912, fine stained glass windows. Corporation treasures include magnificent collection of Irish plate. Business hours, Mon–Fri. Also occasional events, such as theatre.

St Columb's Cathedral (CI), Bishop St. Memorial window depicts lifting of famous siege. Another window honours noted hymn writer Mrs Frances Alexander. Chapter House has historical objects, including padlocks and keys of gates closed by the Apprentice Boys in 1688. Daily, 9 a.m.–12.30 p.m.; 2–5 p.m. Nearby Fountain St has well-preserved wall murals of King William.

St Eugene's Cathedral (C), Infirmary Rd. Gothic style, late l9th century. Fine stained glass. Flamboyant, atmospheric building. Daily.

Long Tower (C): built in 1784 just outside SW of city walls. Lavishly decorated interior.

Gordon Gallery, 36 Ferryquay St. Works by prominent local artists. Daily, 11 a.m.–5.30 p.m.

Orchard Gallery, Orchard St. Regular exhibitions by local artists, also occasional Arts Council exhibitions and workshops, meetings, concerts. Tues–Sat, 11 a.m.–6 p.m. Details, tel. 269675.

The Northern Ireland rail network

1. Bridge End
2. Victoria Park
3. Sydenham
4. Marino
5. Cultra
6. Seahill
7. Helen's Bay
8. Crawfordsburn
9. Carnalea
10. Bangor West
11. Moira
12. Knockmore
13. Hilden

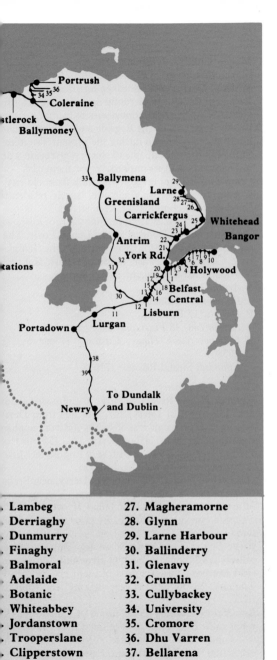

Portrush
Coleraine
34 35 36
stlerock
Ballymoney

33 Ballymena

29 Larne
28 27 26
Greenisland
Carrickfergus
24 25 Whitehead
23 Bangor
22
21
32 York Rd.
31 20 5 6 7 8 9 10
cations   19 1 2 3 4 Holywood
17 18
15 16 Belfast
30 13 14 Central
12
11 Lisburn
Portadown Lurgan
38
39
To Dundalk
Newry and Dublin

Antrim

Lambeg	27. Magheramorne
Derriaghy	28. Glynn
Dunmurry	29. Larne Harbour
Finaghy	30. Ballinderry
Balmoral	31. Glenavy
Adelaide	32. Crumlin
Botanic	33. Cullybackey
Whiteabbey	34. University
Jordanstown	35. Cromore
Trooperslane	36. Dhu Varren
Clipperstown	37. Bellarena
Downshire	38. Scarva
Ballycarry	39. Poyntzpass

Magee College, Northland Rd. Occasional theatre films, other events. Details, tel. 265621.

Walls of Derry: only unbroken fortifications in either Ireland or Britain. Walk round open S sections for fine views of city. See also various cannons facing Guildhall Below W section lie the Bogside and Creggan estates internationally known during the present Troubles.

Shipquay St: walk up one of steepest streets in world to Diamond, with its impressive war memorial.

Craigavon Bridge: invigorating walk from old city to E side, known as the Waterside, largely residential Good exercise climbing the steep streets.

St Columb's Park, Waterside. Fine views of Inishowen Peninsula on Co. Donegal side of Lough Foyle. There are also walks along the quays, through the Georgian style Clarendon St area, in Brooke Park and along Northland Rd towards the city boundary.

S *Acorn,* 3 Pump St.

  Dolphin, 41 Strand Rd.

P *Duffy's,* 17 Foyle St.

  Anchor Inn, 38 Ferryquay St.

R *Counties Steak House,* Customs House St, tel. 265861.

  Strandid, Strand Rd. tel. 271038.

Around Londonderry:

Cumber House Riverside Park: just outside Claudy 8m (13km) SE of Derry; 147, 148 bus from Derry Nature reserve, picnic area on banks of River Faughan

Eglinton: 5m (8km) NE of Derry; 143, 152 bus from Derry. Tree-lined village with very English air. Just S is Muff Glen, with woodland walks.

Old Prehen House: 3m (5km) S of Derry, near Prehen Golf Course; 98, 102 bus from Derry. Various works of art, including portrait of James II, who smiles or frowns according to the light. By prior arr. with Knox family.

River Foyle: S of Derry. Some 4m (7km) of former railway track between bank of river and Letterkenny road has been turned into a pleasant riverside path The city, on the hills, is very striking seen from the river.

Roe Valley Country Park: just S of Limavady. Old water mills from great days of linen trade. Riverside woodland walks, picnic sites. Visitors' centre with exhibition facilities, restaurant. Easter–Sept., 10 a.m.– 6 p.m. daily.

COLERAINE
See Belfast-Londonderry line

UNIVERSITY
Trains stop here during term time only. For details of tours, events, etc. see under COLERAINE (Belfast–Londonderry line).

CROMORE
Formerly Portstewart station. Trains stop infrequently – check timetable before setting out. Also accessible by 140 bus from Coleraine.

Portstewart: 4m (6km) SW of Portrush. TIO Town Hall, tel. 2286. EC Thurs. (except summer). The main streets of this attractive, Victorian-style town form an Atlantic promenade, winding round rocky bays, with shore paths at each end. Magnificent 2m (3km) long strand between town and River Bann.

DHU VARREN

PORTRUSH
Resort town set on a peninsula jutting into the ocean, with attractive terraces and a bustling seaside atmosphere. Railway station of architectural interest. Many summer entertainments, including Town Hall theatre, fishing, bowling, swimming. Good beaches at east and west strand. TIO Town Hall, tel. 823333. EC Wed. Bus enquiries, Coleraine bus station, tel. Portrush 8223/5.

Portandoo Countryside Centre, Bath Rd. Interpretive, information centre, tel. 823600.

Cliff walks W towards Portstewart, E to Dunluce. At E end of chalk White Rocks, picnic area with fine coastal views. Daily summer boat trips leave from harbour, round offshore Skerry Islands:

Barry's, seafront: huge amusement arcade.

S *Coffee Pot,* Dunluce St.

P *Harbour Inn,* 5 Harbour Rd.

R *Rowland's,* 92 Main St, tel. 822063.

Ramore & Lobster Pot, The Harbour, tel. 823444.

Around Portrush:

Bushmills: 3m (5km) S of Giant's Causeway; 138 bus from Coleraine. EC Thurs. Old Bushmills Whiskey Distillery has world's oldest distillery licence dating

from 1609. Attractively set by St Columb's Rill. Mon,
Wed, Thurs, tours at 10.30 a.m., 2.30 p.m. Tel. first
31521. Open-topped Bushmills bus runs from Coleraine to Giant's Causeway, daily, June–Aug.

Dunluce Castle: midway between Giant's Causeway
and Portrush; 132, 138, 172, 252 bus from Portrush.
Magnificent ruins on crag above sea, dating from about
1300. Part of the castle fell into the sea in 1639, taking
with it several unfortunate servants who happened to
be in the kitchen at the time. Two years later it was
abandoned. Today it is one of the most massive and
romantic ruins in Ireland, with spectacular views.

Dunseverick Castle: E end of Giant's Causeway.
Slight ruins of one of Ireland's earliest castles dating
from about 500, perched on a high crag.

Giant's Causeway: 9m (12km) E of Portrush; 172 bus
from Portrush. Ireland's best-known tourist attraction.
A fascinating, often spectacular landscape of six-sided
basalt columns. The tallest, in the Giant's Organ, are
about 36ft (12 metres) high. Information centre, shop.
Also picture boards telling story of the *Girona* (Spanish
Armada Galleon). Café. Bus from car park to Windy
Gap.

Geological walk: 3m (5km), signposted, illustrated
information panels, an excellent way of seeing the
area's geology.

Pleaskin Head: to E of Giant's Causeway. Magnificent
panorama of whole N Antrim coast and parts of SW
Scottish coast in clear weather.

Portballintrae: 2m (3km) SW of Giant's Causeway;
138 bus from Portrush. Pleasant, secluded seaside village with harbour and beach. Boat excursions from
harbour in summer.

Portcoon Cave: N end of Giant's Causeway cliffs.
Beautiful internal colouring, enter from landward side.

Portnabo Slipway: near Giant's Causeway entrance.
Boats to view Causeway coast caves from sea in
summer.

Safari Park: Causeway Safari Pleasure Park, 4m (6km)
N of Ballymoney; 132 bus from Portrush. Lions and
other exotic wildlife roaming extensive parkland. Curio
shop, picnic area. restaurant. Apr–May, weekends
only, June–Aug, daily, 11 a.m.– 6.30 p.m. Details,
tel. Dervock 41474.

Belfast – Larne

BELFAST (York Road Station)

WHITEABBEY

JORDANSTOWN
University of Ulster. Occasional public arts performances.

GREENISLAND

TROOPERSLANE

CLIPPERSTOWN

CARRICKFERGUS
Medieval coastal town with lots of historic interest. TIO, Castle Green, tel. 6360 (end June–Aug.). EC Wed. Bus enquiries, Circular Rd bus station, Larne, tel. 2345.
Carrickfergus Castle: built 1180, in military occupation until 1928. Best preserved Norman castle in Ireland. Now a magnificent museum. Interesting relics of three local regiments and illustrations of numerous episodes in Irish history. Splendid Great Hall, chilling dungeons, fine views from battlements. Apr–Sept, Mon–Sat, 10 a.m.–1 p.m.; 2 p.m.–6 p.m.; Sun, 2 p.m.–6 p.m. Oct–Mar, Mon–Sat, 10 a.m.–1 p.m.; 2 p.m.–4 p.m.; Sun, 2 p.m.–4 p.m. Otherwise by arr. with caretaker.
St Nicholas' (CI), off Market Place: founded in 12th century, four interesting stained-glass windows by

Steam locomotive near Antrim

Lady Glenavy, Catherine O'Brien, Ethel Rhind. Near church, small section of old town wall.

Boneyfore Monument: E outskirts of town. Marks site of 18th-century cottage home of grandparents of US president Andrew Jackson. Restored 19th-century homestead open to public, Apr-Sept, daily except Fri, 2 p.m.–6 p.m.

Dobbin's Inn, High St: 17th-century pub has interesting relics of old town, including huge fireplace. Ask to see secret passage that runs to castle.

Louis MacNeice Plaque, North Rd: the distinguished poet lived in the town from two years of age until he went to Cambridge University. His father was rector of St Nicholas' church. Commemorative plaque on rectory gate.

Guided Walkabout Tours of Town: all year, by arr., Borough Council, tel. 63604.

Carrickfergus Festival: end July/early Aug.

Harbour: just W of castle. Plenty of seaborne activity. Rowing boats may be hired. Walks along the wide promenade and in Marine Gardens.

Shaftesbury Park: walks, putting, etc.

S *Courtyard Coffee House*, Scotch Quarter.

P *Northgate*, 61 North St.

R *Dobbins Inn*, 6 High St, tel. 63905.

Around Carrickfergus:
Kilroot: 4m (6km) NE of Carrickfergus; 163 bus from Carrickfergus. Ruins of church where youthful Jonathan Swift was 18th-century incumbent.

Knockagh Monument: 2m (3km) SW of Carrickfergus. One of the best vantage points in area. Approach by path through golf course, or by road on N side, which runs almost to the top of the cliffs.

DOWNSHIRE

WHITEHEAD

Attractive seaside town with good walks along promenade E towards Black Head, from where you can enjoy fine views over Belfast Lough. The Railway Preservation Society of Ireland (RPSI) has preserved several old steam locos and carriages. Summer trips and excursions to various parts of Ireland. Details, tel. 78567.

S *Coffee and Cream*, 10 King's Rd.

R *Dolphin*, 15 Marine Parade, tel. 72481.

Around Whitehead:
Islandmagee: peninsula 7m long, 2m wide (11 x 3km);

169 bus from Whitehead. Fine cliffs on E side, with the Gobbins (about 200ft, 60 metres) swarming with seabirds. Brown's Bay, Ferris Bay are popular bathing and picnic spots.

Portmuck: N tip of peninsula. Sandy cove and harbour reached by corkscrew road. Ruins of ancient castle, said to have been home of a Magee chieftain, on headland to E. Try your luck with a delicately poised Rocking Stone, a glacial boulder on the rocky shore E of Brown's Bay. Nearby Druid's Chair dolmen.

BALLYCARRY
Quiet hilltop village. EC Sat. Ruins of Ireland's first Presbyterian church, built 1613. Grave of James Orr (1770–1816), poet and United Irishman.

MAGHERAMORNE

GLYNN
At foot of Glenoe Glen. Picturesque village with old corn mill and dam. From old church, footbridge spans River Glynn.

LARNE TOWN
The gateway to the Glens of Antrim. TIO, Victoria Rd, tel. 2313. EC Tues. Three interesting churches: St Cedma's Inver (16th century); First Presbyterian Church, Bridge St (17th century); Unitarian Church, Ballymena Rd (17th century).

District Historical Centre, Cross St. Exhibits include 1900 country kitchen, with open turf hearth, dresser, grandfather clock; old smithy, with anvil, hand bellows, tools, photographs. All year, Tues–Sat, 2 p.m.–6 p.m.

Walks: Chaine Memorial Park, seashore promontory, sickle-shaped Curran promontory S of harbour.

S *Alexander's Coffee Corner*, 38 Main St.

P *Eagle Bars*, 1 Station Rd.

R *Curran Court*, 84 Curran Rd, tel. 75505.

LARNE HARBOUR
Departure point for ferries to Cairnryan and Stranraer in Scotland. Also ferry service to Islandmagee, daily, first sailing 7 a.m., last 9 p.m.

Passengers wishing to travel further north from Larne can take a bus from Larne bus depot to Cushendun, via Ballygally, Glenarm, Carnlough and Cushendall. Details in timetable.

Dunluce Castle, Co. Antrim

Belfast – Bangor

BELFAST CENTRAL

BRIDGE END

VICTORIA PARK

SYDENHAM
for Belfast Harbour Airport.

HOLYWOOD
Pleasant seaside town on S shores of Belfast Lough.
EC Wed.

Old Priory Church, High St: roofless ruins, partly dating from 13th century. Variety of good walks: around back of town, up into Holywood hills; along the esplanade, start of a 5.5m (9km) coastal path to Bangor; from Redburn House, wooded walks, good views of Belfast hills.

Grendor Gallery, 116 High St: regular exhibitions by local artists, Mon–Fri, 10.30 a.m.–12.30 p.m., tel. 4670.

Seapark, by sea-shore, tennis courts and other sports facilities.

   Coffee House, 27 Church Rd.

   ✦ *Old Priory Inn*, Main St.

Spade Mill at the Ulster Folk Museum, Cultra

R *Schooner*, 30 Main St. tel. 5880.

MARINO

CULTRA

Ulster Folk and Transport Museum will provide a very full day out in search of Ulster's social and economic history. Cultra Manor has displays of domestic objects, furniture and crafts, with 19th-century photographs and William Conor paintings. Reference library. In surrounding park, re-constructed rural buildings, city streets, spade mill, linen scutch mill, blacksmith's forge, weaver's house. Transport section documents over 200 years of Irish transport, including the 1893 Carrickfergus-built 'Result' schooner, old aircraft, donkey creels and pony traps. May–Sept, Mon–Sat, 11 a.m.–6 p.m., Sun, 2–6 p.m. Oct–Apr, Mon–Sat, 11 a.m.–5 p.m., Sun, 2–5 p.m. Details, tel. 5411.

S *Manor House*, Ulster Folk Museum. Open museum hours.

R *Cultra Inn*, Culloden Hotel, Craigavad, Tel. Holywood 5840.

SEAHILL

HELEN'S BAY

Small resort on S shore of Belfast Lough. Pleasant walk from the baronial-style railway station to the beach and interesting coastal walk to Bangor. EC Thurs.

R *Carriage*, Station Square, tel. 852841.

CRAWFORDSBURN

Crawfordsburn Country Park has beach, camp site and a shore path forming part of the 'Ulster Way' walk to Bangor.

Crawfordsburn Inn dates from 1614 and retains much of its old world atmosphere.

Clandeboye, Game and Country Fair, June–July.

R *Crawfordsburn Inn*, 15 Main St, tel: Helen's Bay 853255.

CARNALEA

BANGOR WEST

BANGOR

Originally the site of a rich and influential monastery founded in 559 by St Comgall and devastated, three centuries later, by the Danes, Bangor today is a popular, pleasant and prosperous seaside town extending

...ng the sandy bays of Bangor and Ballyholme. ...teresting and pleasant coastal walk to Crawfordsburn ...untry Park. Plenty of indoor entertainments, with ...umber of nightspots, and excellent shopping. TIO, ...e Esplanade, tel. 472092, June–Aug 31. EC Thurs. ...s enquiries: Abbey St bus station, tel. 474143.

...ngor Abbey, at entrance to town, just off main Bel-
...st road: there are traces of the original monastery,
...t most of its stone wall was used in the building of
...e present church in 1617.

...wn Hall, Castle Park: ancient bell of Bangor Abbey
...d facsimile of Bangor Antiphonary, oldest datable
...cument written in Irish 1,300 years ago. By arr.,
...creation officer. The town has a fine arboretum.

...ard Park, on Donaghadee side of Bangor: attractions
...clude nature trail, children's zoo, bowls, putting. All
...ar, daily.

...omenade, complete with traditional seaside amuse-
...ents, sunken gardens at E end, Marine Gardens at W.

...mmer theatre, Central Avenue: full range of enter-
...inments, tel. 475729.

...a cruises, daily during summer at 10.30 a.m., 2.30
...m. and 7.30 p.m. from harbour, weather permitting.

...ckie Pool, outdoor swimming pool on front.

...cycles: G. P. Marshall and Son, Abbey St, tel:
...0467.

...llymacormick Riding School, Ballycormick Rd,
... 458020.

Ca'dora Bakery & Coffee Lounge, 111 Main St.
Humble Pie, 28 Dufferin Av.
Helmsman, 21 High St.
Cavern, Main St.
Skandia, 99 Main St. tel. 461529.
Cartwheel, 44 High St, tel. 456362.
Swaggers, 17 Hamilton Rd, tel. 452072.

...round Bangor:

...allyhome Beach: 1m (2km) stretch on E side of Ban-
...or, with a promenade made for strolling.

...allycormick Point: pleasant shoreline walks at the
...ntrance to Belfast Lough. Enter from the Ballyhome
...d of Bangor promenade or from the Watch House,
...roomsport Harbour.

...roomsport: 3m (5km) E of Bangor; 3 bus from Ban-
...or. EC Thurs. Old-world village with beach and
...omenade. Cockle Row has a summer exhibition of
...orks by local artists.

R *Ranch House*, 49 Main St, tel. 464335.

Orlock Head: 2m (3km) E of Groomsport, mark entrance to Belfast Lough.

R *Whinney Knowes*, 81 Donaghadee Rd, te Donaghadee 883174.

Donaghadee: 6m (10km) SE of Bangor; 3 bus fro Bangor. EC Thurs. A most attractive and relaxing se side town, full of character and characters, built arour an imposing harbour. Good sea fishing.

Autumn colour

Grace Neill's Bar, facing harbour, was built in 16 and happily retains its historic atmosphere. Peter t Great of Russia was entertained here in 1697 durin his Grand Tour of Western Europe. It also sheltere Keats. The laneways in the town centre still have little of the old French-style atmosphere and there a good views of the town and harbour from the castle-lik moat, used for storing explosives during the harbour construction.

Short sea cruises, 10.30 a.m., 2.30 p.m., 7.30 p.n daily in summer.

S *Cabin*, 32 New St.

P *Grace Neill's*, 33 High St.

R *Old Pier Inn*, 33 Manor St, tel. 882397.

Copeland Islands: N of Donaghadee, now deserted Lighthouse Island is a bird sanctuary. Boats fro Donaghadee, by arr., tel. Saintfield 510721.